To Siobhan:
You touch and know the aesthetic truth
that moves all people beyond mortality.
You help us remember who we really are!

. . . I sit before you
  amazed
  that you contain so much
  and are so quiet
  about it.
Gretchen Pfotenhauer Kahn

the power of
creative
writing

*a handbook of insights, activities,
and information to get your students involved*

BERNARD PERCY

A SPECTRUM BOOK   Prentice-Hall, Inc., Englewood Cliffs, N.J. 07632

Library of Congress Cataloging in Publication Data

Percy, Bernard.
    The power of creative writing.

    (A Spectrum Book)
    Bibliography: p.
    Includes index.
    1. English language—Composition and exercises.
2. English language—Study and teaching.   3. Creative
writing—Study and teaching.   I. Title.
PE1404.P4   808'.042'071073   81-4564
ISBN 0-13-687244-1   AACR2
ISBN 0-13-687236-9 (pbk.)

10 9 8 7 6 5 4 3 2 1

Editorial/production supervision
and interior design by Kimberly Mazur.
Cover design by Jeannette Jacobs.
Cover illustration by Mona Mark.
Manufacturing buyer: Cathie Lenard.

This Spectrum Book can be made available to businesses and organizations
at a special discount when ordered in large quantities.
For more information, contact: Prentice-Hall, Inc.
                                 General Book Marketing
                                 Special Sales Division
                                 Englewood Cliffs, N.J. 07632

Prentice-Hall International, Inc., *London*
Prentice-Hall of Australia Pty. Limited, *Sydney*
Prentice-Hall of Canada, Ltd., *Toronto*
Prentice-Hall of India Private Limited, *New Delhi*
Prentice-Hall of Japan, Inc., *Tokyo*
Prentice-Hall of Southeast Asia Pte. Ltd., *Singapore*
Whitehall Books Limited, *Wellington, New Zealand*

contents

preface

In Chapter One, I discuss the benefits and importance of creative writing for the student. What is often overlooked are the benefits and importance creative writing has for the teacher, parent, or whoever is helping a student develop his creative writing ability.

There are many activities required of all of us who are involved with students—activities necessary to a student's education and growth as a person. These activities do bring us personal rewards and satisfactions. Yet helping students develop an awareness, interest, ability, and sense of involvement and commitment to creative writing (or any art form from which they can derive countless benefits) touches educators in a special way.

Faith Delatorre taught English at a junior high school in New York City. Norman was a student Faith could not reach using traditional educational approaches. But one day, during a creative writing lesson, to quote Faith, "Norman came out of the woodwork." He wrote a personal story that so moved Faith that she blurted out with sincere praise, pleasure, and surprise, "Norman, you wrote that?" Faith felt wonderful; she had finally reached Norman.

I remember the first time I was deeply touched, thrilled, and awed by one of my student's written creations. Siobhan was in my fifth-grade class and had written a poem she wanted to share with me:

I hear a voice, I cannot answer.
I hear a song with no last stanza
I see a circle half a size
A horse has won half a prize
All the people have half an eye
I hold a broken pencil in my hand
When I get up on one foot I stand
Somewhere there is my promised land,
But where?

That poem gave me new insight into Siobhan. It helped me understand the depth of her sensitivity, awareness, and thoughtfulness. Creative writing became an invaluable ally for me from that day on. I have featured and highlighted her writing throughout this book. I hope that reading her work—mainly written between 1968 and 1971—will help you find *your* Siobhan Gamble. When you do, you're in for very special and inspiring experiences.

I hope that you, too, choose to make creative writing an indispensible tool. This book is written for you as much as for those students to whom you will be applying its data and viewpoints. May it help you derive the infinite pride, satisfaction, insight, and enjoyment of seeing those you work with become artists—artists who have trust and confidence in you, and in the help and support you provide.

May this book keep you from saying in ten years, "I wish I had known then what I know now."

acknowledgments

One of the great pleasures of writing a book is being able to publicly acknowledge those who have contributed to its creation.

Thanks to Lori Renee Johnson, Lynda Hardy, Roger Jubas, Denise Leto, Julie Himber, Kim Sandoval, my men Orestes Delatorre and Linden Jackson, and Ann Arthur: your viewpoints and written contributions were, and are, greatly appreciated.

Faith Delatorre, Cam Smith Solari, Doris Bell (my wonderful mother-in-law), Kofi Opantiri Williams, Barbara Wiseman, my daughters, Charlene and Kali, and wife, Carolyn: your support, advice, ideas, and inspiration were, and are, valued. Thank you.

A special thanks to L. Ron Hubbard: you contribute so much to so many.

Susan Cambigue, I look forward to many other projects together. Thank you.

Finally, to *all* my former students, from whom I learned so much and who contributed so importantly to this book, please accept my sincerest thanks.

Permission to print the essay *Sleep*, and the excerpt from *Erosinum* given by Orestes Delatorre. All rights retained by author.

John Reps' poem printed by permission of John Reps. All rights retained by author.

Ivanka Samuelson's poem printed by permission of Ivanka Samuelson. All rights retained by author.

Calendar of the Seasons is printed by permission of Carol Sullivan. All rights retained and reserved by Carol Sullivan.

The Great and *Me and My Friends* is printed by permission of Cam Smith Solari, publisher. © 1975. All rights retained by Cam Smith Solari.

Lynette Thomas's poem printed by permission of Lynette Thomas. All rights reserved.

Starting a New Life printed by permission of Carmita I. Cruz. All rights retained and reserved by Carmita I. Cruz.

The Importance of Encouragement written by Beth Wallace is printed by permission of Beth Wallace. All rights retained by author.

Walk Together—Work Together by Ann Arthur printed by permission of Ann Arthur. All rights retained by author.

On Eternal Guilt by Roger Jubas is printed by permission of the author. All rights controlled by author.

Homeboy printed by permission of Brian McCarthy. All rights retained and reserved by Brian McCarthy.

Linden Jackson's poem printed by permission of Linden Jackson. All rights retained by author.

Lynda Hardy's poem printed by permission of Lynda Hardy. All rights retained by author.

Life is printed by permission of Thu Nguyen. All rights retained and reserved by Thu Nguyen.

Ken Seaman's poem printed by permission of Ken Seaman. All rights retained by author.

Robin Watson's poem printed by permission of Robin Watson. All rights retained by author.

Siobhan Gamble's prose and poetry are printed by permission of Siobhan Gamble. All rights retained and reserved by Siobhan Gamble.

Susan Cambique's poem printed by permission of Susan Cambique. All rights retained by author.

My Beginning by Brynn Bishop printed by permission of Brynn Bishop. All rights retained by author.

A Myth on How Deserts Were Formed by William Gary Rogers printed by permission of William Gary Rogers. All rights retained by author.

Matthew Eaton's poem printed by permission of Matthew Eaton. All rights retained by author.

Letty Heldt's poem printed by permission of Letty Heldt. All rights retained by author.

one

creative writing:
an all-purpose tool

To start, I am going to ask you to become a contributing writer for this book. On a sheet of paper, write your definition of creative writing.

In the past sixteen years I have come across many ideas of what creative writing is or should be. There are several with which I heartily agree. One is by B. Maybury:

> (Creative writing) is concerned with encouraging children to use fully what they have within themselves: ideas, impressions, feelings, hopes, their imagination, and such language as they can command. It is an attempt to get at the nine-tenths of the iceberg of a child's mind that he does not often use. . . .

The following definitions are by students who have been or are actively involved in creative writing:

> Creative writings are the expressive thoughts that flow from one's mind onto the piece of paper.
>
> Lori Johnson

> The pencil is the melody. The paper is the music. A poetic mind sets the lyrics. When set together, they stand to create the most beautiful song

ever perceived by the eyes. That is my interpretation or definition of creative writing.

Lynda Hardy

I believe that creative writing is a technique used to state one's thoughts and feelings. In short, I'd say that it is the ability to express a person's imagination in a manner that creates a picture in one's mind.

Linden Jackson

As you read the book I am going to ask you to do three things, to be willing to:

Rethink your personal viewpoint on what creative writing is.

Revise your viewpoint when appropriate.

Maintain your viewpoint when that seems best.

Your personal belief of what creative writing is will obviously affect how you teach and involve students in a writing program, so it is vital that you have clarity and certainty in your personal definition. It is my intent that this book will help you attain or enhance this clarity and certainty.

how students benefit
from creative writing

Here are two reasons why we should write creatively:

The forms of things unknown, the poet's pen/ Turns them to shapes and gives to airy nothing/ A local habitation and a name.

William Shakespeare, a well-known writer

I still can't believe it. . . .I'm good at something and the world knows it.

Chrystal Kornegay, a not-so-well-known ten-year-old writer who said this after a book she helped write was published and nationally distributed

As you read the following material (based on research, experimentation, common sense, and the reports of various people actively involved with creative writing, including students, parents, and teachers) relate your personal experiences to the ones discussed. Try to remember situations in which you received or observed someone else receiving similar benefits from creative writing.

a tool for self-expression

Cervantes wrote, "The pen is the tongue of the mind." If that is true, then creative writing provides the ink for the pen.

Can you remember a time when you felt so moved by something—your love for another, a moment of despair, the beauty of a mountain lake—that you were bursting with the need to communicate your feelings? I'm sure we all have, and students do, too. For some, the best means of expression may be music, dance, painting, sculpture, acting, or comedy; for others, it is writing.

I was recently watching a television show about parents who had to cope with the death of a child. One parent commented, "I never realized how deeply affected my teen-age son was by the death of my daughter. He never verbally expressed his hurt, and I have to thank his high school English teacher for helping me get a better insight into how he was feeling.

"He wrote an essay for his English writing class about the death of his sister. It was a very moving, deeply felt and thought-out essay which his teacher shared with me. Only after reading his composition did I fully realize the extent my son was affected by my daughter's death. Writing was his outlet; he could not express his feelings any other way."

Here are two examples of a child's deeply felt thoughts expressed through creative writing. This first poem was written by an eleven-year-old boy to his family, two days before he died of leukemia. It was written while he was feeling much pain and discomfort.

This poem has a very special meaning and value to Michael's family; it was part of his legacy of love.

The second poem is a channel of communication from a boy to his divorced parents.

The time has come,
my Job is done, now it's
~~The~~ Time ~~is~~ for a
nother one, The gates
will open, open soon

I now will go.
See you soon.

Time, Time will never
stop, Everlasting time,
Love, Love is Eturnal,
Fouever more Love I will
always love you.   .

michael
zacarias
2-11-80

Here I go for another day
I come home
I go to school
I come home
There they are
my parents
Delightful people in many ways
but I just don't know how
to tell them
I try in many ways
but I can't
They fight and argue
nothing seems to stop them
When they ask, I can't tell them
it's hard it's hard
Step by step it slowly goes
I don't know why
but it's gone now
All gone
I wait and I wait
till the right time
but it's too late
My parents are apart
and I've been trying to tell
love to my parents
All gone all gone
I awake to another day
hoping it will happen
But my fantasy is all gone all gone
I am sad but there is nothing I can do
but I will still love and wait.

John (12 years old)

Sholem Asch said, "Writing comes more easily if you have something to say." I know we all have something to say, even if it's to only one other person. It is up to us to help create writing programs to allow students to say what needs saying.

a tool for understanding

The act of writing is a time for a writer to reflect, to play around with ideas, to gain new and deeper insights into what he or she feels and believes; it's a time for him to polish the things about which he wishes to write, until they become clear and understandable communications.

To illustrate the above, here's an exercise for you. Think what it is you truly like about someone close to you. Think of someone, perhaps that person, to whom to communicate your thoughts, then go ahead and share them.

Did you find you were able to polish your thoughts and feelings about that person? I hope so.

In a very real sense, the writer writes in order to teach himself, to understand himself, to satisfy himself . . .

Alfred Kazin

Imagine how Siobhan, who created the following poem, had to work through and explore her feelings and beliefs before she could communicate what was really on her mind.

Black

Black—It's just a color,
Black—doesn't mean a thing,
Black—makes so much trouble,
Black—was Martin Luther King
Black—got beaten for it,
Black—had to take it too
Black—always the bad color
Black—rarely politely "a sir" but "Hey you"
Black—you all can't learn to read or write
Black—just cause your color ain't light
Black—I just came out to be that way
Black—and Black I'm gonna stay!

a tool to help develop
personal satisfaction, pride,
and a feeling of self-worth

How often do we underestimate the value of what we do and the effect what we do has on the lives of the students with whom we work? How often has something we've done, or involved a student in doing, had an important impact on that student of which we were not fully aware?

The answer to both those questions is a very definite "many, many, many times."

Creative writing is a wonderful tool for providing opportunities that have a meaningful impact on the life of a student, very often in ways we don't perceive. I would like to share a personal anecdote that illustrates some of the benefits a student can gain from creative writing (benefits that are not always apparent).

This story concerns Jerry, a ten-year-old who was in a creative writing workshop I conducted.

I strongly believe in the importance of having students share their written creations with others. A technique I use with great success is personally selecting and reading samples of writing by various students; I don't tell who wrote the selection. At the end of the reading class is to guess who the writer is; after five guesses I ask the writer to identify himself by standing or waving his hand, if he wants (the writer always has the right to remain anonymous).

I did this with a story Jerry had written, an excellent piece of writing. When the class was asked to identify the writer, no one mentioned Jerry's name; he was one of the poor academic achievers in class and everyone thought, "He couldn't be the writer of this great story." As the class was mentioning the names of other students they thought had written the story, I glanced at Jerry, who was fighting to restrain his smile. He realized how much the class liked what he had written.

When I asked the writer to stand, almost everyone looked at the two top students in the class. There was a moment of disbelief when neither stood, and then all heads turned and spotted Jerry standing at the back, a huge smile on his face.

I didn't realize how great an impact that experience had had on Jerry until I spoke with his mother a few weeks later.

She told me, "I don't know how you did it, but Jerry has never been so enthused or involved in any school activity as he is for writing. He even puts a small table in his closet, turns on the light, warns everyone not to disturb him, and closes the door and writes. It's really terrific to see him so involved and excited. Thank you."

The feelings of pride, satisfaction, self-respect, accomplishment, enthusiasm, and the belief in one's ability to create are some of the benefits awaiting those who are part of a well-thought-out creative-writing program.

Take a moment and think back to a time you created something that truly pleased you. Get in touch with all your feelings at that time. A nice remembrance, isn't it?

Help provide many such remembrances for the students with whom you're involved; creative writing is a wonderful tool to help you do that.

a tool for increasing awareness and perception of one's environment

Peace is:

A kitten all warm in a mother's warm fur.

Everything floating in the sky and you feel warm.

Looking at the hills, and they grab you and say peace.

A cold night, sitting by the fireplace feeling the warmth.

Sitting on the front porch, listening to the robins, cardinals with their alto voices.

Being all by yourself on a gliding cloud.

Enjoying the cool breeze that is coming to your face.

Kittens sleeping softly in a box of softness.

When the pillow whispers to you to have a good night.

A white boy and a black boy shaking hands.

The feeling of running through a sheet of grass on a hot summer's day.

Something that brings you into it.

The preceding are excerpts from essays written by students in the fifth grade. They were asked to observe their environments and look for things that help remind them, or give them feelings of, peace. I think you'll agree their responses were most perceptive and varied.

How many of us go through life at least half-blind to the world around us? When was the last time you really observed something using all the perceptive abilities you have? Any three-year-old child can be a wonderful teacher when it comes to understanding how to observe one's environment; his intensity and commitment to observe what interests him is inspiring.

At some point today, pick out something to observe in your environment—your child, a tree, a building, the sunset—and observe it from the viewpoint that this will be the last time you will ever perceive that thing. Decide how you can express to others what you observed.

Creative writing can be a wonderful tool to help heighten a student's sensory awareness and develop his powers of perception—on physical, emotional, and spiritual levels.

a tool for active involvement, not passive acceptance

Have you ever had the "joyous" experience of sitting for five hours watching TV, being a passive receiver, with ideas and communications only flowing in? It's almost like being dead. Schooling is too often a similar situation, in which the student is basically a passive receiver.

An activity like creative writing helps reverse this passive, sometimes apathetic, state. It allows the student to outflow, create and be actively involved.

What about your schooling? In which activities did (do) you take part that really excited and interested you? I'll bet the vast majority were activities in which you were actively and creatively involved in some way.

Jane Rollins, a fourteen-year-old high school student, commented, "I get wiped out taking in, taking in, taking in all day long. I need a break to put out knowledge and feelings to someone else."

Creative writing provides the perfect opportunity to "put out knowledge and feelings" to somebody.

a tool for developing an understanding of and ability to use the language

The attainment of literacy (that is, the ability to read and understand what others have written and the ability to use words through writing to transmit information and ideas to others) is probably the most universal purpose of schooling. Creative writing can be an invaluable tool in helping children become truly literate.

reading and creative writing

The Great[1]

I am pretty and charming and handsome. I am a lady. I know how to cook eggs. I wear false eyelashes and lipstick.

by Rosemary

This short descriptive paragraph was written by a student in a third-grade remedial reading class who was a non-reader. She became involved in a special reading program in which creative writing was used as a major tool to teach reading.

Cam Smith Solari, who taught the class, made these comments:

Creative writing certainly works at helping children learn how to read.

It puts a child in a better position to learn, because he is actively creating, not passively receiving information.

The words he writes belong to him. He knows them and since we all use the same language he can read those words when others write them.

One final point. When you work with a group, the children will have a great interest in what other kids have to say and want to read their written creations, even to the point of asking the writer what certain words are.

How creative writing can be used to help teach and develop reading skills (as well as other curriculum areas) will be covered in

[1] In Cam Solari, ed., *Our Class Book: The Greatest Stories in the World* (Los Angeles: © 1975 by Cam Smith Solari) p. 97.

more detail later. For now it is sufficient to state that creative writing can motivate, involve, and help create a greater understanding and enjoyment of reading.

I've noticed that, in the past few years since I have started writing seriously, there has been an increase in my interest in reading, my appreciation for the writing of others has heightened, and my increased understanding of how the language is used has improved my comprehension of what others write. These same kinds of benefits await others who become active writers.

communication and creative writing Creative writing helps develop a student's ability to use language as a means of expression and communication (both verbal and non-verbal). It's a basic truth that if you wish to really know and understand something, you should actively do or use it. Learning to use language is no exception.

As a student writes, he becomes more aware of and interested in words, the building blocks of language. As he decides such things as the best word to use, the words that go together best, and different ways thoughts can be expressed, a student develops his ability to understand and use words for both practical and creative purposes.

Here is a charming example of how language can be used by a child who understands it. Justin is the nine-year-old son of a friend of mine. He had been gathering up his nerve for two weeks to call a girl in his class on whom he had a crush. He finally mustered up the courage to call and spoke with her about whatever it is that nine-year-olds discuss.

After hanging up the phone he rushed to his mother and joyously came out with this beautiful line, "Mom, I just spoke with you-know-who and I *feel a rush of relationship.*" Isn't that a great description?

Here is another example. Beth, a former student of mine, wrote the following when discussing parent-and-child relationships: "Many people look down on kids, and it's not because we're short, either."[2]

Creative writing can immeasurably help a child learn how to use language to express what he wishes or needs to communicate.

---

[2]Bernard Percy, ed., *How to Grow a Child: A Child's Advice to Parents* (Los Angeles: Price, Stern & Sloan Publishers, Inc., 1978) p. 14.

two other benefits
from creative writing

One of the nice things about writing is that *it is inexpensive and anyone can do it on his or her own level of ability and sophistication.* Creative writing also *helps develop initiative and self-discipline* as a student learns to start, continue, and successfully complete an assignment or project in creative writing.

an embodiment of creative writing

What Is A Child

A child is a person full of many
wonders and ideas.
A child can express reason in
family discussions and
decisions.
A child is a person worthy of the
warmth of love and affection.
A child should be taken seriously,
respecting his desires and
dislikes.
A child is a person who shouldn't
be pushed in a direction that
he doesn't think he would
enjoy or be happy in.
A child is a person who learns
from the surroundings he
lives in,
And those surroundings should be
of love, trust and understanding.

Lori Johnson[3]

This poem by a twelve-year-old student embodies much that creative writing has to offer.

[3]Percy, p. 20.

12

It helps a writer focus his attention on a particular subject, leading to increased awareness and understanding of that subject.

In addition, a writer grabs on to those concepts and images he already has, or will be developing, as he focuses on what he will be writing about. This in turn leads to a further understanding of the subject.

Creative writing helps to develop cognitive (thinking) skills. As a writer organizes his thoughts, decisions are made on how to best communicate what it is he wants communicated. He decides which ideas are relevant and which are not.

a final word

Creative writing is truly an all-purpose tool. How it's used depends on the needs, interests, and purposes of the writer *and* the teacher.

I would like to close with a quote from a former student of mine, who write, "I'm new to the world of writing, but it certainly is exciting."

It sure can be!

two

about creativity and art

Afternoon In Virgo

The music comes sweet to me,
Like my lover's breath
Enchanted, I absorb
Its delicate vapor
Floating all through my mind
Swirling and merging
Like liquid smoke
In rainbow hues
I close my eyes
And dance all around inside

Siobhan Gamble

For me, one of the most wonderful things an artist's creation can do is cause me to "dance all around inside."

As an educator who has been intimately involved in the creative arts, I know with certainty that *all* people have the innate potential to express themselves and create in any art form. Through my under-standing of what creativity is, and what art is, I am better able to help people move closer to achieving their creative and artistic potentials.

The purpose of this chapter is to help you generate your own thinking about and clarify your understanding of creativity and art; this understanding is really a prerequisite to the teaching of creative writing or any art form.

Susan Cambigue—dancer, poetess, educator, creative artist in the truest sense of the word—has written two essays that form the basis of this chapter. The thoughts and viewpoints she expresses are more than just words to Susan; they are testimony to how she lives and works.

creativity

> Creative thinking may mean simply the realization that there's no particu-lar virtue in doing things the way they always have been done.
>
> Rudolph Flesch

To best understand what creativity is requires personal aware-ness and involvement in the creative process. I would like you to re-spond to some questions to help you look at *your* personal awareness and involvement.

What do you consider creativity to be? Do you consider yourself a creative person? Why, or why not?

How do you express your creativity?

What was your most satisfying creative experience?

Basically, creativity involves an individual responding in her own way to the ideas, images, sounds, relationships, and other stimulations found in her past, present, and future environments. It is tuning into her own channel and being the writer, director, and actor in an original script; it's being true to her own ideas and thoughts, which results in a personal creation.

Creative thought begins with alertness, observation, and an abil-ity to allow mental pictures and thoughts to flow freely and interrelate in the consciousness of the individual. It is a point of view and a way of thinking that affects all aspects of life.

Unfortunately, many people do not allow themselves to think original thoughts; they have been conditioned to view things in only one way. Too often they have suppressed their original thoughts and viewpoints because of invalidation by others (others making them seem wrong or making less of the things they do and feel), fear of ridicule, and pressure to accept the viewpoints and ideas of various authority figures (teachers, parents, peers, "experts," the popular view).

The role of the teacher is to teach, guide, motivate or enhance his or her students' ability to observe, become aware of what they observe, and express in creative form what is felt and known as a result of that observation.

The creative process begins by focusing attention on a problem, idea, feeling, or scene. When this happens, the senses respond and feed the individual a variety of information, which often leads to a brainstorming process, with a flow of mental pictures and thoughts rapidly coming into view. These provide the individual with a potpourri of information. This process must be allowed to flow freely, with no discussion, evaluation, or in-depth look at each item of thought; later thoughts can be looked at, explored, and separated so one idea can be developed as expansively as desired. (Approaches to develop this brainstorming technique, a cornerstone of creative thought, are presented in Chapter 10.)

Another view of the creative process is evidenced in this anecdote about Anton Bruckner. Someone asked him, "Master, how, when, where did you think of the divine motif of your Ninth Symphony?" Bruckner replied, "Well, it was like this. I walked up the Kahlenberg, and when it got hot and I got hungry, I sat down by a little brook and unpacked my Swiss cheese. And just as I open the greasy paper, that darn tune pops into my head!"

Bruckner's attention was not consciously focused on finding that tune, yet his training as a creative artist caused his attention to be focused on finding that tune at some level of awareness. When it jumped into view, he was ready for it.

If the creative process involves anything, it is being ready to create with that idea, tune, image, or visual scene when it jumps into view.

art

what is art?

Artists can color the sky red because they know it's blue. Those of us who aren't artists must color things the way they really are or people might think we're stupid.

Jules Feiffer

Art can be viewed as the combination of knowledge, perception, and creative thought refined in an expressive form. Writing, dance, drama, music, and the visual arts use different senses to communicate a point of view.

One of my former students wrote that art is "the release of personal thoughts, fears and emotions . . . It's self-expression . . . it holds a special secret for every individual."

What is your definition of art?

the arts as a problem-solving method of thinking

Art can be the result of an inspiration, perception, search, or expression of a strong emotion. Most often it is the product of creative problem-solving. An example in visual art would be the work of French artist Claude Monet, who was absorbed with the concept of light and its effect on color. He would paint the same scene many times at different times of day or in different seasons in order to explore the dynamics of light and color.

One of the best examples of a problem-solving approach in modern dance is that of choreographer Bella Lewitzky, who takes an idea and explores it inside and out in order to discover new information that is then selected, developed, and refined into her innovative and unique choreographies.

In creative writing, the process is similar. Both the student and the professional need to find the word combinations that will capture and communicate the impact and quality of their thoughts. This is a process of exploration, discovery, selection, and evaluation.

17

the arts and education

"To lead forth or to draw from within" is a basic meaning of the word "education." This concept of "drawing from within" has been weakened, for much of today's education stresses the learning of skills rather than the development of originality. When school budgets are cut, the arts are usually considered expendable rather than the "basic skills." However, it is the arts that help each person expand as an individual and teaches her a process of thinking that enables her to solve problems and best apply the basic skills learned. So it is the combination of basic skills and creative thought and activity that results in the most effective education for a student.

Another point to consider is that there is a tendency in schools to encourage, even pressure, students to conform their individual thoughts to the "right" thought or answer. This often results in students suppressing their own abilities to solve problems creatively. They may also lose skill and confidence in their abilities to view themselves and the world around them from their unique point of view.

The creative arts can reverse this process, with creative writing one very effective means of helping students regain, learn, or enhance their ability to look at themselves and the world around them from their unique point of view—stoking the imaginative and artistic coals which are waiting to be fired.

Rousseau stated, "The world of reality has its limits, the world of imagination is boundless."

Probably the most rewarding part of any art form is when the artist can give expression to his dreams and put them forth into the world of reality. I would like to share a poem written by Susan Cambigue when she was hovering between her imagination and dreams and the reality of the world.

When on the earth, the sky
portrays a surreal mist of
unknown heights.
When in the sky, the earth
conveys a surreal mist of
unknown depths.
Perhaps what fills the space
between earth and sky holds

the visions which we seek.
Reality is where we are.
Visions lie just beyond that point
of direct focus.

Take a moment and think of a dream that is important to you—
something you wish to see become reality.

Now visualize your dream and see it actually occurring.

A nice feeling, isn't it, bringing the dreams of imagination to the
actuality of existence?

Teachers should help bring their students' dreams of imagination
to the actuality of existence, to nourish their students' artistic souls.

As Ruskin said, "All that is good in art is the expression of one
soul talking to another and is precious according to the greatness of
the soul that utters it."

three

the basics for motivating and involving students in creative writing

I would like to share something with you. I have been writing and rewriting this chapter for a couple of weeks; it has been a real effort to complete this section of the book. About twenty minutes ago I realized why I have been stuck in creating this chapter; I was overlooking the simplicity of what it takes to involve and motivate students of all ages to write creatively. What sparked the realization was an experience I just had with Charlene, my three and one-half-year-old daughter.

For the past twenty minutes I have been enjoying Charlene's company. She was sitting in my lap as we listened to some mellow jazz and the sound of a Los Angeles rain as it touches the ground. While I held her in my arms, her head gently resting on my chest, I was thinking how to best begin this chapter—perhaps the most important in the book.

I thought of Charlene's smile, joy, and insistence that I read one of her recent written creations: I ⁊⁊ ℰ ℥. To Charlene that was as fine and important a creation as anything ever written by anyone, anytime, anywhere.

I recalled the pride and satisfaction of thirteen-year-old Reggie Wright, a former student of mine, after he had completed the following poem:

Dig Yourself

Dig yourself, beat on my head.
Dig yourself, my clothes are all red.
I see beating if I did something wrong,
But every night it's the same old song.
First with a mop handle, then with a broom,
Before I know it, Pow! Bang! Zoom!
And if you get me on the floor,
You don't stop you want more.
JUST BECAUSE YOU HAD A BAD DAY,
YOU TAKE IT OUT ON ME IN EVERY WAY.
This isn't punishment, this is cruel
If you want my opinion, it just ain't cool.[1]

I remembered the thrill and pleasure of a very close thirty-eight-year-old friend, after she had written her first book.

Those written creations were born and developed out of the following basic principles, which should be applied to anyone learning and becoming involved with creative writing, whether that person is three and one-half, thirteen or thirty-eight.

basic principles that encourage and motivate creative writing

Lori Johnson, a former student of mine, wrote, "A teacher should encourage a student to express her own thoughts, to motivate her to reach into her mind and write whatever she is thinking, and to arrange her innermost thoughts in a way that others are able to see where she is coming from."

Here are some key ways to help encourage and motivate a student's writing:

create a safe and validating environment   This is an environment in which a student feels free to let others know him as he really is, feels, and believes. To create this environment, make a student feel that

[1]Percy, p. 38.

having expressed himself is "right" and help him feel good about what he has written. I'm *not* saying you have to agree with, or even like, everything he creates, but you should avoid making the student feel that what he has written, and the fact he has written, is wrong or no good.

Simply stated, make a student feel that expressing his feelings, thoughts, and viewpoints is all right. This will help the student believe and know he has something to say that other people value and are interested in.

Can I Speak Of Love

Can I speak of love–do I have
*   the right?*
Do I know how it is to feel
*   fiery passion in the night?*
Do I know how to kiss and feel
*   my lips on fire?*

Siobhan

To answer Siobhan's first question, *yes*, you have the right to speak of love. You have the right to speak of anything you wish.

allow a student to be causative and self-determined in his creative work   It's the student's creation—his thoughts, feelings, images, beliefs, and experiences; you can guide and suggest, but always allow the creative artist, the writer, to decide what and how to change his creations. Always give him belief in *his* ability to create.

My attitude went from feeling I had the right to change a student's creation because "I knew better," to feeling I had to convince a student to do it the way I felt it should be done, to biting my lip, clenching my fists, and counting to 1000 by ½'s to keep from trying to impose my viewpoint. But I finally reached the point at which I could make suggestions when the student was ready and willing to receive them, recognizing that the student had the total right to decide about any changes to be made in his creation.

help the writer expand his knowledge and understanding of his environment and vocabulary   Talk, explain, question, discuss, point out, demonstrate, listen, experience (by direct participation, observation, imagination, or discussion).

Writing comes more easily when you have the words to say what you want to communicate.

encourage experimentation with words and value unique ways of expressing oneself   Allow students to stumble and be awkward, wrong, inappropriate, nonsensical, or outrageous in their use of words; eventually students will polish their diction and come up with gems in their writing, like these lines taken from the writing of two former students of mine:

A swift wind can dim the light that glowed for years.

Ann

Are tears worthless—when you cry over silly things?

Siobhan

help students write towards a goal; give them or help them find a purpose with which they agree   "OK, kids, write about, 'If You Were a Doorknob.' Discuss how you would feel; you have forty minutes. Start!"

Some students may approach a "you-*must*-write" type of activity with eagerness, but it can too often lead to protests (no matter how silent) and become a turn-off for writing.

One secret for really involving students is to give them, or help them find, a meaningful and relevant goal they wish to attain with their written creations—the best work will be published in a class magazine, see how funny you can be, really try to express exactly what you feel. One student wrote, "My teacher stimulated my interest in creative writing by drawing it out, asking for my involvement in another successful project (a book that got published)."

practice your preaching   If students see *you* write, and you share your written creations with them, it will invariably help involve them in creative writing.

The following poem is by Ivanka Samuelson, a superb teacher who knows how to motivate and involve students in creative writing. Her poem reflects the truth and importance of practicing what you preach.

We teach children
We preach expression,
extension of self.

Yet isn't it funny
as adults we conceal.

We teach children
We preach exposure of feelings,
"Let go, it's all right" we say.

Yet isn't it funny
as adults we draw a curtain.

We try, we pound
We extract, we discuss
We write, we probe.

Yet isn't it sad
adult's feelings are silent.

take advantage of a student's interests and abilities   In the words of an anonymous sage, "When you have the interest and ability to do something, it gets done."

How well do you really know and understand the interests and abilities, beyond the realm of schoolwork, of the students with whom you work? Think about your students and mentally, or on paper, list what each student's interests are and what each student is good at doing.

I am amazed how often I failed to study my students' interests and abilities in depth. Too often, I let the various teaching pressures and responsibilities get in the way of my truly knowing and understanding my students, much to both our detriments. Yet every time I learned how to better work with my students, we both benefited.

I had a student, Donald, whose goal seemed to be to write as little as possible as few times as possible—until I discovered his "passion" in life.

Sometime after the start of the school year, he became interested in science fiction; he became a "trekkie"—a devotee of the TV show "Star Trek." I discovered this when I asked the class to write an essay on "who you would like to be lost with while riding the New York City subways" (I figured subways would be more meaningful and relevant than a desert island).

Donald wrote a three-page essay, writing on both sides of the paper; I couldn't believe it. He did a wonderful detailed analysis and commentary on why he would like to be lost with Mr. Spock, a character on "Star Trek."

Donald and I spent much time enjoying his written creations that centered on science fiction.

Knowing and using the interests and abilities of students will be a powerful ally and tool of any teacher.

create opportunities to have students' written work read by others (but only when the writer agrees)   I remember the first time something I wrote was read and liked by other people; it was in my third-grade class. I was on top of the world and couldn't wait to write more things to be shared with others. The pride in having *my* work enjoyed by others was, and still is, a real thrill and motivation for me.

In answering the question "What is your fondest memory related to creative writing?" one student wrote:

> I guess the recognition that I've received from being a writer is what I'll remember most. Especially when I won a "brotherhood composition" contest. I wrote the essay so that it would be good, not just so I could win. Winning was a big surprise. I think it even surprised the audience that a black girl in a predominantly white school could win. In a weird way I felt that I had proven myself.

> Ann Arthur

Recognition is a powerful tool.

All the above points are very basic. However I have not yet mentioned the two most basic and necessary viewpoints to help involve and motivate a student to do creative writing:

1. FAITH AND BELIEF IN EVERY STUDENT'S ABILITY TO WRITE CREATIVELY.
2. ENTHUSIASM IN HELPING A STUDENT DO CREATIVE WRITING.

I've never met a student who was incapable of writing creatively, but I have met many people who couldn't unlock (or would lock up) the creative interest and ability of students.

I very strongly suggest, if you do not believe with certainty in your students' ability to write creatively, and you do not approach creative writing with enthusiasm, *do not* involve yourself with it. Find someone else who possesses those viewpoints to teach creative writing to your students.

Ann Arthur wrote, "Look into your child and you shall see your reflection."[2]

If you look into your student you will also find your reflection; let it be one of faith, belief, and enthusiasm.

what now?

I'd like you to take a moment to reflect on the following:

Can you remember a time you felt the joy, satisfaction and personal pride that came from being able to help a student develop his potential into an actual expertise?

Can you remember a time you felt the frustration, upset and dissatisfaction that came from being unable to help a student—who was ready, willing and able—develop his potentiality?

Success, or failure in working with children is dependent on your ability to answer the question, "What Now?"; a question we must constantly ask and be able to answer if we intend to help students develop their true potentiality.

I would like you to read this excerpt from a letter written by a former student of mine:

> I need all the information on young writers that I can get my hands on. You see, presently I am gathering the courage to tell all those concerned that I don't intend to be a doctor, nurse, or lawyer. These are the professions I am being urged to consider . . . The only thing that I'm really interested in is writing . . . I remember when I wanted to be a psychologist and a politician, I was talked out of it. Not this time, I'll only quit if I discover it's not for me . . . Life is too short to waste time . . . With my luck I'll be at the typewriter the rest of my life.

[2]Percy, p. 36.

What now? What can and should be done with someone like this student who is interested in writing, especially creative writing? What now?

is teaching creative writing possible?

Can good writing be taught? . . . If you're talking about 'creative writing,' whatever that is, the answer is an emphatic *no*.

Jefferson D. Bates

For creative writing to flourish, it is especially important that the teacher be a receptor rather than a direct giver, and a guide rather than a dictator.

Grace K. Pratt-Butler

Is your answer to the title question a "no," or a qualified "yes"? I say a qualified "yes." The basic tools of writing—the rules, techniques, vocabulary, stylistic elements, and ideas that help make writing crisper, clearer, more precise and more easily understood—can be taught. The understanding of the creative process—what it is and how it can be used in creative writing—can be taught. A teacher can provide the tools, help create the environment, help stimulate a purpose for writing. But a teacher cannot endow a student with the creative potential that is inherent in the spirit, soul, karma of everyone.

A teacher cannot provide or teach this creative potential; he can help provide tools, ideas, information, rules; help a writer develop certain skills and attitudes; help create an environment in which students feel safe to write creatively. But it is a student's creativity—her uniqueness as an aesthetic being—that will determine how she uses what she has been taught and knows.

six major purposes
in teaching creative writing

Your purpose in teaching creative writing may vary when working with a particular student, class, or activity. At times you may be a teacher, receptor, guide, inspirer, evaluator, critic, editor, or whatever you find you have to be. By knowing your purpose for involving a student in a specific creative-writing experience, you will know your role and plan of action. Your purpose is based on your judgment and understanding of what students need and/or want.

Following are six purposes you may find yourself using, separately or in combination, in your teaching of writing:

1. *To introduce a student to a specific style and form of writing.*

When teaching, I invariably come across a student who loves to write "roses-are-red" poetry such as

> *Roses are red,*
> *Violets are blue.*
> *Sugar may be sweet,*
> *But not you too.*

That's all he would write because he had never been exposed to any other form of writing that he had both enjoyed and mastered.

One of my responsibilities, I believe, is to introduce students to a variety of writing styles and forms, helping them know and understand how to use these to communicate their thoughts, feelings, and ideas.

My goal is to ensure that students have the knowledge and ability to express themselves through the essay, haiku, cinquains, "roses-are-red," limericks, the short story, one-act play, or whatever writing style and form they find to their liking and appropriate to their needs and purposes. Actively presenting a variety of creative-writing forms and styles, and helping students master the ones that really interest them, are major responsibilities of any creative-writing teacher.

After reading the following excerpt of a free verse poem by a twelve year old student, I'm sure you'll agree she has the knowledge and ability to express herself.

Calendar of the Seasons

In Autumn
watching the red-gold leaves
as they drift
softly
to the ground,

brings to mind
bits
and pieces of remembrances,
memories
from the past.

Bits from family walks,
crunching on leaves
and,
how the days grow cooler
and cooler,
settling
into the crisp, spicy days
of October
and November.
Thoughts
of Halloween,
of trooping the streets with
witches
and ghosts
and goblins
and tramps,
of pounding up steps and
knocking on doors
and shouting
"Trick-or-treat!"
and going home with
a bag
full
of candy
and apples
and popcorn

and sometimes
home-baked fresh cookies.
Memories of watching
full yellow moons
rising
slowly
into
the night
seeming to catch in the branches
of trees
bare of leaves,
of turkey
and cranberries
on Thanksgiving
blending
into the vivid colors
of Fall.
And then
you remember seeing
the beauty
of the first
soft, white
snowflake
of the year and realizing,
suddenly,
that it is Winter.

Carol Sullivan (age 12)

2. *To help students practice and master a writing skill, rule or technique, currently or previously taught.*

Writing is a craft as well as an art form, and knowledge of its rules, skills, and techniques, and how to use them, is essential. A teacher of creative writing should, at times, help writers improve their writing craft. What is of concern is not the overall quality of the written creation but improving the ability of writers to know and understand how to use the tools of their craft.

For example, follow up a unit on descriptive words with a writing activity that uses descriptive words; have students use their editing skills to rewrite a wordy 350-word story into 150 words.

3. *To have students use their writing ability to communicate their thoughts, feelings, and understandings about some area of interest and concern.*

To help accomplish this purpose I use the following stages of activity (how, when, and if you help students will vary from situation to situation):

a. Help students decide what they want to communicate. The topic of their writing can come from anywhere—what they enjoy, what they dislike, what their attention is on, a problem they have, how they react to something in their environment. The important thing is that writers find what really interests and concerns them and find a purpose for writing about that subject or theme.

For example, the following poem touches a major area of interest and concern felt by Siobhan. Her purpose for writing the following is evident. (This was written during the late 1960s, when Black awareness, consciousness, and efforts for improving the self-image of Black people were dominant themes.)

Us Colored Folks

Us colored folks
Don't know a thing
All we's good for is
To work and sing
Stupid and ugly
Stink and loud
I'm a colored folk
And I sure am proud

b. Help students decide precisely what they wish to communicate about that subject. This stage concerns helping students focus their attention on a feeling, a problem, an idea, a visual scene. As students focus their attention, a flow of information, ideas, feelings, questions, and understandings will occur. From these the students will find some thing(s) they would like to develop and write about.

At this stage, students are essentially being observers; either through first-hand participation (for example, playing handball); personal observation of something or someone else (for example, watching others play handball); observation of known experiences related to the subject (reading or talking to others about playing handball).

c. Help students decide what form of written expression to use. When students have decided what they want to communicate, the next decision becomes which written form to use: poetry (free verse, haiku, cinquain, limerick), short story, fable, essay (expository, argumentative, narrative, descriptive), play, or a combination of these.

Part of a creative-writing teacher's responsibility is to help writers become aware of as many tools as possible, so they can reach into their "tool bag" and select the best one with which to communicate. Their choice of writing style and form is a part of the creative process.

d. Help create the time and space so writers can write. Some teachers have special writing corners; some classes have a special quiet time of the day when no noise is allowed and each class member can use the time for whatever needs to be done in a quiet environment; some students find a quiet spot in their home community or school where they feel free to think and create.

e. Help students edit their written creations. Once a student has completed his first draft, it's time to proofread and make whatever changes and corrections are needed. This is covered extensively in the following chapter.

f. Help students share what they have written. If students wish to allow others to read what they have written, it's the teacher's responsibility to help them find the opportunity and means of doing that. A class newspaper, a bulletin-board display, and reading to the group are but a few of the ways writers can share their work.

4. *To use creative writing as a vehicle to help students learn and understand various curriculum areas.*

Creative writing can be used as a way of motivating, introducing, reviewing, applying, or practicing various things learned in other curriculum areas. The teacher's concern is to have the writer use or become familiar with facts, concepts, skills, and thoughts found in other subjects covered in school.

For example, a child can write a story using numbers that are multiples of six; create a myth that explains the arrangement of the nine planets in the solar system; write an essay that illustrates how a reporter's use of words can influence how we feel about a news story.

5. *To use creative writing to help students question, gain new insights and understanding about themselves, others, and their environments.*

The following poem by Siobhan reflects her attempt to understand something, the apparently meaningless destruction of something very dear to her in her environment.

> *They cut the tall green bush*
> *in my backyard today.*
> *I found out as I came into*
> *the kitchen–they looked*
> *farther away*
> *I gave out a "hey!" and ran to the window*
> *Why??*
>
> *I've seen the sparrows chirp in that bush*
> *I've seen it bow to the rain and wind.*
> *I've seen it bloom with the first of*
> *spring*
> *I've seen the bees gather and buzz busily*
> *around*
> *Now they're cutting it to the*
> *ground.*
> *I can see the young sprouts*
> *I can see them fall*
> *I don't think there's any*
> *reason at all.*
> *As I look out the window, I can't*
> *help the tears—*
> *It's been there for quite a few*
> *years.*
> *Now—they're tearing it down—*
> *Why??*
> *I DON'T KNOW.*

They cut the tall green bush
in my backyard today.
CHOP, CHOP, CHOP, CHOP.

When you ask students to focus in on themselves, others, or their environments, you really help to expand their personal understanding and awareness. Here are a few ideas to use: What four things bring you the greatest personal pleasure; describe, in exactly 37 words, something you never noticed about your mother; describe two things you never before observed in your house.

6. *To help students create something that will bring them joy, satisfaction, and pride.*

I recently had the experience of doing a creative-writing program with visually handicapped children. At the end of the project their teacher helped put together a book based on the writings and thoughts of each child in the class. Two copies were professionally bound and placed in the school library. Each child was given a personal copy of the book. Their pride, satisfaction, and delight in having helped create that book is something they will always carry with them.

I remember when my first book was published; I took it with me everywhere I went. It was amazing how creative I was in finding ways to introduce my book to anyone I happened to meet. I was most pleased and proud, and I wanted to share my accomplishment with anyone and everyone.

Creative writing offers an infinite variety of ways to help anyone experience the pride and joy of creation.

haiku as an example

Taking haiku as an example, we can see how each of the six major purposes of creative writing may be approached.

1. Introduce haiku as a form of poetry that can be used by the writer.

Teach haiku as a seventeen-syllable poem with a usual line pattern of:

line 1—five syllables

line 2—seven syllables

line 3—five syllables

The subject matter often concerns things of beauty and nature.

The major concern of the teacher is that a student knows the rules for writing a haiku poem.

2. Use haiku to review and practice the use and understanding of syllables.

Having taught the concept of a syllable, haiku is an obvious and fun way to help students master their understanding of syllables.

An easy way for students to identify a syllable is to have them place one hand on their chins and say words aloud. Each time the chin moves down, a syllable has been spoken. (A syllable is a pronunciation unit of a word.)

3. Use haiku for expression of feelings and thoughts.

Siobhan wrote this poem, a variation of a typical haiku theme:

> *The ghetto is dirt*
> *It is trash, and filth and hell*
> *I know how it is*

4. Use haiku as a vehicle for the development of other curriculum areas.

For geology, haiku can be used to describe a desert:

> *The hot desert sand*
> *The rolling heat of the dunes*
> *Lizards thirst for food*

For biology, the physical characteristics of a bird can be described; for language arts, the concept of syllables can be reviewed or introduced.

5. Use haiku to gain new insight and understanding in some area of concern and interest.

You can have students observe something, the way a cloud moves, for example; have students express their feelings about the wind; have students look at those things they may not have previously reflected upon or observed.

When a writer, based on what he has observed, feels he has come up with something to communicate, help him use haiku to express his thoughts and feelings.

Siobhan has written:

> *The sun is shining*
> *Its golden warmness fills me*
> *I'm a child of earth*

6. Use haiku to bring joy, satisfaction, and pride to students.

The validation, acknowledgement, and sharing of the poem a student has created will help bring that precious inner and outer smile to the writer.

It's important that students understand what they are to have as a result of their creative efforts. Your responsibility is to know what you want emphasized, where to direct the students' attention, and what you expect as a final product of the creative-writing activity; in short, to know your purpose.

two essentials
for achieving your purpose

It's essential that you do two things to help your students attain your intended purpose:

communicate the purpose of the writing activity   Your students' knowing which of the basic purposes you have as the teacher, instructor, guide, mentor, catalyst, critic (or whatever term you care to apply to yourself) will help the student writers focus their attention, energy, and skills.

For example, the writer aware he is basically to practice using colorful and descriptive words will be given a clear-cut direction in which to focus his knowledge, experience and understanding—finding and using colorful and descriptive words.

get the writer's agreement to take part in the activity   This is vital. Avoid having to enforce participation in creative writing (or any other creative activity). Each student must maintain his own determination and responsibility when it comes to involvement in the creative arts—or else they become the "enforcive" arts. Enforcing involvement is the best way to turn off a student's creative drive and energy.

To get a student's agreement to take part in the creative writing activity, help him see the personal benefits he can gain from taking part in the activity.

What benefit is needed and wanted will vary from student to student, activity to activity, class to class. But know with certainty that, to the degree a student is aware of, and in agreement with, the benefits he will gain from being involved in some creative-writing activity, the more interested he will be in taking part in that activity.

The creative arts should not be attempted unless they bring benefits to participants.

Siobhan wrote, "Poetry became a strong and beautiful way to make a statement on something. I found it challenging and emotional."

Help your students find their own reasons for creative writing.

four

criticism, evaluation, and editing

I would like you to do two things in connection with the following chapter:

1. Read the following poem, created by a fifth-grader, written and shared with me on her own initiative; then answer the questions below, first before, then after reading the chapter.

2. Observe whether there are any changes in your viewpoints and ways of criticizing, evaluating, or editing, after having read the chapter. If so, what were they?

The Boy

"There's a little boy;
Who lives in a house
Who'se parents are dead.
He went to his aunt
but she said "Go away."
So he went to his
father grave and said
"Oh daddy I
shead a tear, and every-

time I do I get smaller,
and, smaller all the time.
Oh how I wish
I was with you.

1. What would be your comments to the student who wrote the poem?

2. Would you correct the errors in spelling, grammar, and word usage? If so would you correct the errors on the student's paper or would you have the student correct them?

3. Would you have the student change the poem in any way? If so, what would you change? How would you go about having the poem changed—would you tell the student what changes should be made or would you ask the student what should be changed?

4. What kind of questions, if any, would you ask the student?

5. Would you deal with the poem differently if it had been done as part of a class assignment or activity, as opposed to having been written (and shared) on the student's own initiative? If so, in what way?

What are the changes in your viewpoints and ways of criticizing a student's written creation after having read the chapter?

criticism: beware (and be aware), it can destroy

Before going any further I would like to present two definitions of criticism that have relevance for those of us working in the area of creative writing:

1. Criticism is the act of making judgments or evaluations; the determination of the "goodness" or "badness" of something; the reasons why something is good or bad, right or wrong.

2. Criticism is the act of getting someone to do something the way you, the critic, want him to.

To best understand what criticism is, it is vital that you understand what the result of criticism should be, especially when teaching creative writing (or any of the creative arts).

After you have criticized a student's written creation, that student should want to write more, for he should know he's becoming better and more able at communicating his thoughts, feelings, beliefs, knowledge, and truths through creative writing.

The result is *not*, as the second definition would lead you to believe, getting a student to do—write—something the way the critic wants him to. The following poem is relevant to this sort of critic:

> *As a child he thought, I'd love to become wise.*
> *He did not, so began to criticize.*

Criticism, or evaluation, of someone's creative work can be productive or destructive, depending on the way in which it is handled and presented.

In workshops on the creative arts, during my discussion of criticism, I tell a personal anecdote which invariably rekindles memories of similar experiences which most everyone in the workshops have undergone. As you read the anecdote I am pretty sure you too will, unfortunately, be reminded of a similar destructive incident in your creative past.

In June of 1956 the entire 8th grade was rehearsing our graduation songs. The teacher in charge, who shall be named Mr. @#$%¢&, announced that he was going to walk behind each row of students and if "I place my hand on your shoulder while you are singing, you WILL NOT sing during graduation, you will mouth the words with no sounds leaving your body."

I knew I would never feel his hand on my shoulder. I enjoyed singing and was sure I sang well (this was before the wide-spread use of tape recorders, and I had never heard my voice recorded). As Mr. @#$%¢& approached behind me, I gave him little thought. I was happily singing, when suddenly I felt Mr. @#$%¢&'s hand not only touch my shoulder, but his fingers were digging deeply into my flesh. He wanted to make sure I got the message.

I was devastated.

Whatever enjoyment I derived from singing was shattered, and even today I am still somewhat hesitant to sing in the company of others.

After hearing my voice on tape, I must admit that I am not the world's most talented vocalist, but Mr. @#$%¢&'s criticism was unnecessary, poorly handled and left me scarred far beyond what he had intended, causing me to withdraw from singing and music for years.

Bring back any memories? I hope not.

Take a look at the other end of the critical spectrum. Can you remember a time when a teacher, parent, or friend helped you achieve greater success and a more positive attitude toward some area of the creative arts by their statements or actions? A nice memory, right?

There is no doubt that the creative works of students can be improved—that is, that the students can better use the mechanics and skills of an art form to improve the quality of what and how they wish to communicate through that art form. Helping a student improve his artistic creations may require criticism or evaluation from you, but that criticism has to follow certain guidelines. Otherwise, twenty years from now that child may well remember you as a Mr. or Ms. @#$%¢&, the person who helped squash her enthusiasm and involvement to create in a certain art form.

six guidelines for criticism and evaluation

1. *Never, ever tell a student, or even imply, that his honest effort at creation is wrong or no good.* What right does anyone have to tell a student who has created something of which he feels proud that his creation is no good, or to in some way make that creation any less than the student feels it is? After all, criticism and evaluation in the creative arts is only opinion, and I must admit I have much hostility for someone who does not grant a student (or anyone) the right to his feelings of pride and success at creation. You or I may not like it, but someone else may think it is great. What is important, and do not lose sight of this fact, is how the student who created the work of art feels.

Grading creative writing is asinine. All marks serve as is some arbitrary indication of the opinion of the person doing the grading. How it helps a student by giving him a 'C' for creative thought is beyond me.

Based on countless discussions with students, the only real effect of grading creative writing is to turn students off and destroy their enthusiasm for writing.

Those of you who believe in grading: What grade would you give this poem by a third grader?

Me and My Friends[1]

Me and my friends
they had a fight
and they were fighting
all the night
and all the morning.

Robert

What grade does this next one "deserve"? It's by a sixth-grader.

Senryu

How does the ground feel
Being stepped on by peoples feet?
I know it hurts bad.

Lynette Thomas

I really don't understand how I could give a grade to either poem. The first was written by a boy who was a non-reader until he became involved in a creative writing program. His poem, "Me and My Friends", is a wonderful achievement.

The "Senryu" poem is by a girl who is considered gifted. To me her poem is as fine an achievement as the first.

Aesthetically I prefer the Senryu poem. What effect would it have on the third grader if I gave the Senryu poem an 'A' and his poem a 'C'? It could only serve to tell him his creation is not as good as the Senryu. I do not see the need to compare his creation to any other; not if my goal is to help involve him in creative writing. Why do anything that would make him wrong, or tell him his work is no good? Why?

[1]Cam Smith Solari, *Our Class Book: The Greatest Stories in the World* (Los Angeles: Cam Smith Solari, 1975), p. 43.

2. *Get the student's agreement to be evaluated.* Do not force your evaluations on a student; let him agree to hear your critical opinions. Put yourself in the student's position; are you always willing to hear criticism of your work and creations?

3. *Allow the student to maintain his self-determinism, causative-ness, and responsibility for his creation.* There are essentially two sides to criticism. On one side are those evaluations and judgments in which the critic is in agreement with what the creative artist has done; there is little if any problem with this. On the other side are those evaluations and judgments in which the critic is not in agreement with what an artist has done—that is, the artist has done something the critic feels should not have been done or has not done something the critic feels he should have. This is the side of criticism in which a critic must exercise care, restraint, and good judgment.

Creative efforts can certainly be improved, and you may see a way to achieve improvement. In making those suggestions (only after the artist has agreed to hear your considerations) keep these points in mind:

a) Let the artist know you are expressing *your* feelings, and that *you* feel what he has done can be improved. This way you let the artist know you are evaluating how *you* feel about the creation. By doing this you allow the artist to maintain a causative, self-determined viewpoint on his creation, and he knows he has the right and freedom to decide on any changes to be made.

b) Do not tell him what he has done is wrong, unacceptable, or poorly done. This way you are evaluating and invalidating *him* as well as what he has done. This tends to place him in a position in which he may feel he does not have the right and freedom to decide whether to change his creation, but that others have the right to decide for him.

c) Make suggestions in the form of a question or how you, the teacher would change things if it were your creation. For example, "I might use the word 'angry' instead of 'perturbed' " or "How would it be if you used 'angry,' not 'perturbed'?" By doing this you give the artist the freedom and space to determine for himself whether to make a change.

4. *Find and indicate what you feel is good and right about a creation as well as what you feel could be improved.* The more "right" you make a student feel for what he has done, the more willing he will be to listen honestly to your suggestions for improvement. The more "wrong" you make what a student has done, the more eager he'll be to have you get out of his life and creations, turning a deaf ear to your suggested improvements. He will fight to make himself right, even to the point of not creating anymore.

5. *Help the student develop the necessary skills, understandings, and knowledge to evaluate his own creations.* Your responsibility is to know the correct questions to ask or have the student ask about his creation. For example: Does it really communicate what you intended? Is the description of the character too wordy? Would a metaphor be appropriate here? Is the story interesting to read or boring?

6. *Keep the teaching of the required skills of an art form separate from the creative process and efforts of a student.* For years I was guilty of doing what I am telling you *not* to do. When a student writes something from his creative soul, do *not* mark it and correct it for spelling, grammar, punctuation, word usage, penmanship, plot development, characterization, or wrong rhyming pattern. Make a note to yourself what skill the student needs work on, and by all means work with him on it. Correct him as needed but *not* as part of a creative effort he has turned in.

How would you feel if you just showed your friend something you had written, a poem of which you were really proud, only to have your friend start talking about how your first sentence needs a "juicier" verb and that "me" should never be used as the first-person pronoun after the verb "be." I would love to have that person write ten thousand times, "I will not criticize when it is not requested or wanted." All that friend should really do is read the poem, understand it, and acknowledge your creation.

I shudder to think of all the former students who endured my red-pencil marks on their creative efforts. I wonder how many of them lost their motivation and inspiration to write because I felt I had to correct their skills, not just acknowledge their creations.

I now apologize to those students.

If you *must* use a red pencil, underline and circle the *good* and *positive* qualities you find in the creative writing.

a safe environment

One of the most important things anyone can do to foster creative writing is to create an environment in which a student feels safe and free, with the confidence and trust to take chances and communicate through writing whatever is important to him. The key is to make a student feel right and *always* allow him to be self-determined about his creation. Any criticism or judgment that does not truly foster these goals is destructive and has no place in the creative-writing process.

If criticism helps a student know all the accepted rules and mechanics of being a good writer as well as how *you* feel things should be done, but its effect is to destroy any desire or intention to write (as so often happens), then the criticism is really a crime against the student.

I was once observing a class whose teacher had students stand as she read aloud their creative-writing assignments. She proceeded to point out all the things that were wrong about the stories. I still cringe at the stupidity and arrogance of that woman. I made a point of meeting each of those students whose work had been torn apart by that woman (she does not deserve to be called a teacher), and told each of them what I *liked* about their creations. Wouldn't you be reluctant to do any creative writing in her class?

Criticize and evaluate, but keep these points in mind:

1. Never invalidate a student by telling him his creative effort and work is wrong or no good.
2. Get the student's agreement to have his work evaluated.
3. Allow the student to maintain his self-determinism, causativeness, and responsibility for his creations.
4. Find and indicate what you feel is good and right about a creation, as well as what you feel could be improved.
5. Help the student knowledgeably criticize and edit his own creations.
6. Keep the teaching of the required skills and mechanics of creative writing separate from the creative process.

To end this section of the chapter I would like you to answer the following question. Which definition is appropriate for your style and intention of criticism?

1. Criticism: The art of impressing someone with how little he knows, and how unable he is.

2. Criticism: The art of impressing someone with how much he does or can know, and how able he is.

The creative efforts and future of the students with whom you work may well be determined by the way you handle and present your criticism. How would you now criticize the poem at the beginning of the chapter?

editing creative writing

Editing is the process in which the editor (student or teacher) adds to, deletes from, changes, or makes no changes in a written creation.

As H.G. Wells wrote, "No passion in the world is equal to the passion to alter someone else's draft."

I have been both the victim and victimizer of this passion. On July 10, 1979, you might have heard a heart-searing scream emanate from my home in Los Angeles. That was when I first read the changes the copy editor wanted to make in my book *Help Your Child In School* (Prentice-Hall, 1980). "What the @#$$%¢&#$$%@@# does she think she's doing to my creation?" I thundered. I was more than outraged and I did not suffer in silence (as my wife can attest).

After my initial emotional response, I reread the copy editor's suggested alterations and had the good sense to differentiate between those alterations that really were needed and helpful and those that were not.

I wonder how many of *my* victims (part of my outrage at the copy editor was colored by my realization that I had victimized far too many of my former students because of my passion for alteration) felt the same anger I did, yet suffered in silence and finally decided they couldn't, shouldn't, or wouldn't involve themselves in creative writing.

The goal of editing should be based on a passion for helping a writer improve the quality of his intended written communication, not on a passion for alteration.

Francis Bacon wrote, "Reading maketh a full man, writing an exact man." I would like to add to that, "Editing makes a *more* exact man."

The teacher of creative writing should be concerned with knowing the why (goal) of editing, when to edit, what to edit, and how to edit.

why edit

The goal of editing, whether by the student, the teacher, or by both, should be to help create a more precise and concise aesthetically written creation which clearly communicates what the writer intends, in the way he intends it.

when to edit

If I were . . .

If I were a ant. A boy named Patrick he step on me. I bet his toe he went home and tell his ma. He take a wood but he don't remember me because I went home he kill all my friends and I come out and bit on he's finger now he only have 7 finger he never see me again.

There are obvious places to edit this work, ways that could enhance the story and its communication, and help the writer develop important writing skills; yet I chose *not* to edit this paper until two weeks after it was written and presented to me.

This was one of the writer's first voluntary attempts at creative writing, and I felt that accepting and acknowledging his creative effort, flow, and product was of paramount importance. He was very sensitive to criticism and I did not want to intrude on his sense of pride and satisfaction at his accomplishment by editing and teaching the rules and techniques of writing.

After he handed in several other creative efforts in the following two weeks, I felt he was ready and secure enough to edit his first paper. His sensitivity and personal stake in the story was lessened by the added success and validation he received for his other work.

I asked him if he would like his paper edited for display in the classroom. Only after he agreed did we begin to edit the paper.

The judgment of when to edit should be based on your perception of such things as: what the student needs to know and do to improve his craft as a creative writer; his probable willingness to hear and accept evaluation and viewpoints on what to edit; his likely willingness to act on the data and viewpoints discussed or presented.

The key thing to remember is *not* to do anything that would lessen the student's involvement, interest, and growth as a creative writer.

I do not discount the need and value of editing a student's creative writing. A teacher's guidance and instruction is invaluable and necessary for a student to achieve increased mastery of the craft and art of writing. What I am stressing and warning about is that the creative psyche—the spirit—can be a very fragile thing, easily prone to damage.

The amount of creative talent that has been quashed, invalidated, suppressed, and destroyed by someone's "well-intentioned" editing and teaching of the rules and mechanics of writing (or any art form) is incredible. Two basic reasons for this have been a teacher's not knowing when to edit or help a student edit his writing and/or the enforcement of editing and the teaching of rules and mechanics to the creative-writing student.

edit when the student agrees on the purpose for the editing   Part of your responsibility is to help a student see and agree on the need and purpose for editing her written creation. Find a reason to which the student can relate, and with which she can agree, that would motivate her desire to have her work edited. For example: to be put on display somewhere, to be read to the class, to be sent out to a magazine for possible publication, to be put in a personal creative work folder which will be made into an anthology, to help her learn how to improve future written creations.

It is essential that you *do not enforce* the editing of a student's creative work!

The ultimate goal is to get a student actively involved and interested in editing his work, not passively sitting there, grinding his teeth and tightening his jaw, as you force him to edit his creative work.

edit when the student understands what and why something he wrote needs editing   To help a student understand requires two things. First, the student needs to know and understand that the purpose of editing creative writing is to help create a more precise and concise aesthetically written creation which clearly communicates what he intends, in the way he intends it.

Essentially you want the student to observe for himself how effective editing can be for improving the quality and effectiveness of a written communication. At first, use other people's writing, starting with short writing examples that need editing. For example, use an overhead projector and show a poorly written paragraph on the top half of the projection with an edited version(s) on the bottom half. The type and difficulty of the example will depend on the needs, interests, ability, and sophistication of the student(s). For fourth-graders of average reading ability, you might use a paragraph like this:

1. *Original:* Bill was scare. This I think, you should really really know is going to be the first time ever he asked Joan to accompany him somewhere on a date.

2. *First edited version:* Bill's knees kept hitting each other as they shook. This was the first time he ever asked Joan out on a date.

3. *Second edited version:* Bill was scared. This, you should know, was going to be the first time he ever asked Joan to go out with him on a date.

(It might help generate interest and enthusiasm if student's names are used in these selections.)

You can also show examples of your own written creations before and after editing, discussing how the editing helped improve them.

Second, the student needs to know what (and how) to edit. Your judgment again comes into play. Your decision of what the student needs to know and practice is based on: his and/or the class's needs, interests, abilities, and sophistication; the form of creative writing done—poetry (which kind), story, essay.

Editing skills are based on a knowledge of what to look for when editing writing. Volumes have been written about this; books on essential writing skills and on how to edit abound (see Bibliography).

The student should concentrate on two areas when editing his work: the mechanical rules and techniques of writing (the basic writing skills), and the aesthetic flow and style of his written creation.

what to edit

Here are some of the basic writing skills and viewpoints of which one should be aware when editing.

1. The organization and arrangement of ideas and data:

Putting material (facts and ideas) in a correct sequence of order.

Putting ideas in logical groupings.

Showing the relationship, when necessary, between various ideas and facts.

Presenting appropriate supporting details and concepts for the main idea(s).

Ensuring that the writer sticks to the theme—main idea—of the written creation.

2. Presentation of material:

The use of concrete and realistic examples and illustrations.

The tone (humorous or serious) of the writing.

The use of appropriate diction (choice of words)—formal or informal English, euphemisms, hackneyed expressions.

The preciseness and conciseness of the writing (avoid wordiness).

The overall clarity that helps the readers understand what's been written.

The correctness of spelling.

The use of transitions (words, sentences, and paragraphs that help bridge the written work, creating a smooth flow from one idea to another—"in addition," "however," "first," "second").

3. Grammatical considerations:

Are the sentences complete (not run-ons or fragments)? Written with their parts (words, phrases, and clauses) clearly placed and understood?

Are correct punctuation and capitalization used? Are the first words of sentences begun with capital letters? Are commas used to set off parenthetical expressions and items in series? Are periods and exclamation and question marks appropriately used?

4. *Personal and aesthetic reaction to the writing:*

What effect(s) does it create for you (intellectually, emotionally, and spiritually)?

What do you feel about the choice of words, form, and style used?

Is the writing vague or definite?

Is what's communicated relevant and meaningful to you?

How does the overall presentation feel (pleasing, boring, exciting, or interesting)?

There are specific points to look for when editing the various forms of writing—poetry, stories, essays (see relevant chapters for more information on editing each form).

charts and checklists

You can use a variety of charts and checklists to help a writer know what to look for when editing—for example, this list of the qualities of a good essay.

1. The basic theme is understandable.
2. The writer's purpose is understood.
3. The writer sticks to the subject.
4. The writer clearly develops (organizes) the subject material.
5. The presentation is effective.
6. The essay creates a meaningful and relevant response from the reader.

helpful hints on editing
creative writing

develop a student's editing skill on an appropriate gradient Work with short, easy pieces and go on to more complex and involved revisions when teaching the skills of editing (revising). Have the writer focus on a small, limited number of things to edit; then as his skill, knowledge, and ability grow, expect more from the writer and help him focus on as many areas as are appropriate. With a student new to editing, you might help her use more descriptive words in one sentence, while a more advanced student could work on the entire written creation.

Be careful not to overwhelm and confuse a student by asking her to confront more than she is willing and able to do.

select specific techniques and skills to develop The decision on what techniques and skills to develop will be related to the student's writing skills and the form of writing being edited. If the form is poetry, specifically couplets, you might help the student develop skill at hearing and writing consistent rhythmic patterns.

When you evaluate in order to help a student edit his written work, find specific things to communicate and to which you want to direct the writer's attention—don't just say "great improvement," but say "Your use of descriptive words to describe the man is much improved." (This could even be broken down further, by identifying the descriptive words and why they help the writing.)

as needed, work together with the writer, but at times, let the writer work independently Always apply the basic viewpoints presented in the last chapter on how to criticize and evaluate—especially maintain interest, warmth, and acceptance of the student and his written creation.

edit with the viewpoint of helping the writer find out how much she knows, or can know, and how able she is One way of doing this is to help a student concentrate on what's right about his writing, then indicating, in appropriate ways discussed earlier, perhaps one or two areas in which there could be improvement.

T.S. Eliot has stated, "An editor should tell the author his writing is better than it is. Not a lot better, a little better."

What would you tell Siobhan, and how would you help her edit these poems she wrote? The first was written when she was in fourth grade, the second when she was a junior-high-school student.

God's Creation

God created us, that's what they say,
He made us good in every way
He gave happiness throughout the world
He gave parents to every boy and girl
Boys and girls grew, their babies were born
But still, all in all, we all must mourn
If God created us so good and kind,
Why has man such an evil mind?

Night

A haze is falling
the sun's brilliant anger is
slowing down
The bird cries lonely
The dim-gray squirrel scampers
nervously—
The cats eyes gleam with a new tomorrow—
it is night.

The streets are lively
People rushing, running rapidly to
their hard-earned rest
Button coats—pull up collars
Turn on the car lights
Get the kids inside—Tomorrow's school
it is night.

Watch television
do homework on the kitchen table
Move your little sister off
the chair
Don't open that window—it's gonna
drop to 19 degrees tonight—
pull covers up tight
it is night.

five

the essay (composition)

an essay by Siobhan

Think

Just to think, right now, a new born baby is shedding its first tears, beholding its new world as it can only see fit, and its mother rejoices, or does not hear its welcome or cries too, but not for you.

To think, an old man, helpless as a baby, is passing away—just a regular nap for one so old, but this time forever.

To think—a soldier—on the battle field, young and bewildered—not hating—yet killing—in a war not his own. From a non-sleeping sleep—the sleep of a wary dog—he is awakened to a dawn to protect and defend himself—his country?

Or to think, still in the dawn—an early hunter's gun pierces the breast of an elk—a golden tiger—a giant moose—a great eagle—to hang its majestic head on a plaque where all can see.

To think—a child—hungry. Why hungry with a stomach so large? Why then is not the rest of him large—but skin and bones. Right now he is crying or fighting for the carcass of a dog—or maybe for his brother. And to think of his mother—he has none—never had one and never will.

To think—this minute of a poor woman with children hungry, with children cold, with children roofless and children unwanted by society—not cared about—not thinked about.

To wonder—to ponder about the white man, Red man, Black and Yellow man—The four legged animal, the two legged one—The trees, grass, water—the LAND—The Earth. There's much to think about. *So much* more than I have said—But *have* you thought? If you have, what have you *done?*

Siobhan Gamble

Why include a section on the essay or composition in a book on creative writing?

The answers can be found in Siobhan's essay. If that is not an example of creative writing I will personally devour every page of this section. The writing of essays, or compositions, involves the writer's interest and involvement in some topic, leading to personal observation and study which results in a new or more complete awareness and understanding of that subject. It involves a writer's decision of how best to express and communicate what she wants through the medium of the essay, experimenting with the various forms of essay and language use. It involves the originality of what and how a writer decides to communicate on that subject.

what is an essay?

. . . the essay perhaps the freest of all types of prose.

Francis Connolly

An essay is basically a short literary composition, usually written in prose on a specific subject or theme.

To understand what an essay is requires an understanding of its purpose and the purpose of the writer. Charles Townsend Copeland has written, "Whenever we encounter the typical essayist, he is found to be a tattler, a spectator, a rambler, a lounger, and, in the best sense, a citizen of the world."

Siobhan's essay clearly shows her care, concern, and willingness to work for the improvement of the quality of life. Siobhan is truly a citizen of the world. She has communicated her information, feelings, beliefs, observations, experiences, and concepts to you, the reader, with the intention of increasing your awareness and understanding and getting you to think, clarify, and react in some way to the subject of her essay. (That's right, she did *all* that.)

What Siobhan has done is to fulfill the purposes of an essayist: dealing with the reality of this world; presenting or interpreting facts, concepts, ideas, and experiences that actually exist; conveying a sense of what is, what has been, or what could be. The essayist instructs or indicates truths and beliefs as she sees, feels, and understands, in order to create an increased understanding, awareness, and/or response by the reader.

why involve students in the writing of essays?

The reasons a teacher helps involve students in the writing of essays can vary. Writing essays:

> can help the writer develop cognitive skills as she observes, researches, solves problems, selects, organizes, evolves, and develops the material she'll write about in the essay.

> can help the writer better understand and become more aware of the material he is writing about.

> is a way of reaching out to, touching, and communicating with others.

> provides all the benefits discussed in the chapter on how students benefit from creative writing.

The following material on the essay will present some helpful facts and viewpoints that you can apply as needed to your creative-writing students in order to help them achieve growth as writers and citizens of the world.

the styles of essays

There are two general writing styles in essays:

Informal essay—Siobhan's is an example of an informal essay. What comes through the writing is her personality; it's a free-form style of writing.

Formal essay—This is the "bananas are yellow and grow on a tree-like tropical plant" type of essay. The focus is on the subject, which is presented in a straightforward, conventional style of writing.

And there are four basic types of essay:

The *expository* essay essentially explains or conveys facts and ideas. It's written in a clear, definite format.

The *descriptive* essay basically reveals or suggests a picture, the physical appearance of some person, place, or thing. It tries to create a picture (image) in the reader's mind.

The *argumentative* essay attempts to persuade or convince the reader to accept an idea, viewpoint, attitude, or belief. Attention is given to illustrating the truth or falsehood of some thing. The writer's purpose may be to motivate the reader to action.

The *narrative* essay tells a story or presents a series of events in the order in which they occur. Its purpose is to give meaning to an event, or series of events, by telling a story.

The expository is the most common form of essay, but essays often include elements of two or more of these types. For example, touches of narration and description can help vitalize an expository essay.

Read the following composition on sleep by twelve-year-old Orestes Delatorre, and observe the style and type of essay it is.

Sleep

Sleep can sometimes be regarded as a kind of drug, too little will make you stagger or nod, too much can dope you up and promote headaches quite a bit. Children are prone especially to these irregularities, since they nap.

NAP; the very word arouses a slight fear in a child's mind, since they want to be included in everything you (as a parent) do. The child may fight the sleep; but in the end, he/she can't help but konk out.

However, if you've ever wondered why a child is so cranky after a nap, try this theory: While the child was asleep, he/she missed out on errands or activities you participated in. The child is crying because he feels left out, he knows you were doing things while he was asleep, and he did not participate in these activities.

So when your child wakes up cranky and crying, try filling him in on all the things you did while he was asleep; it just might help.

things to consider when choosing the topic for an essay

1. is it meaningful and relevant?

I was doing a creative-writing residence in a school and wanted to help the children become familiar with the essay, especially expository and descriptive essays. My efforts were met with the same enthusiasm you would expect for a six-hour homework assignment given on the next-to-last day of school. I was valiantly searching for something which would spark the class. I joked, prodded, pleaded, asked, probed, trying to find something meaningful and relevant to this unresponsive group.

"Have you thought about careers?" (Silence.)

"What interests you?" (Deathly silence.)

"Your favorite foods are . . . ?" (Absolute deathly silence.)

"Tell about one another." (A glimmer of enthusiasm; three girls looked up at me with a gleam in their eye, looked around at the rest of the apparently comatose class and decided, "Forget it.")

Out of frustration, but with a smile, I said, "It would take Bruce Lee (the martial artist-movie actor) to get you to do anything like this."

Eureka!! A response. Three kids jumped out of their seats and assumed a karate attack position. The class laughed and I said, "These guys could star in 'Enter the Lizard.' " (Bruce Lee was currently starring in "Enter the Dragon.")

There was an outburst of laughter. I had found the area to which the class responded with interest and enthusiasm. Now I had to probe for that bright idea that would direct their interest towards writing essays.

One girl called out, "Bruce Lee, he's OK, but Jim Kelly, he's the main man."

There was soon a cross-fire of argument as to who was the number-one karate man. Several names were being argued about.

The light bulb switched on. The essay should be an argumentative type, not the expository-descriptive one I had originally planned. There would be a vote to determine the number-one tough guy after all the essays were completed. The theme would be, "Why _____ is Number One."

The class was involved; they had a purpose to which they could agree, and they wanted to know how to write an argumentative essay.

We discussed the things to include in an argumentative essay: give evidence (facts) that support your viewpoints; be specific; build your argument point by point, based on your own observations and understandings. The class had a great time writing their essays and arguing who was number one. (Bruce Lee won out over all his competition.)

The key points of this anecdote? The topic of the essay should be as relevant and meaningful to the writer as possible, with the writer choosing the essay's topic and deciding or agreeing on what her purpose is for writing the essay. The purpose could be to enter an essay contest; to learn about some part of a subject that interests her; to help others learn what she knows about a subject; to convince others to do something.

The responsibility of the teacher would vary, depending on what the writer most needs and wants. The teacher could work to ensure that the writer is motivated to write, in agreement with a perceived purpose for the essay; could help motivate the writer by working with him to find a topic that will be based on subjects, activities, events, or interests that have meaning and relevance for him.

Unless this first step is successfully completed, the writer being enthusiastic and willing to write about a specific topic, the succeeding steps are doomed to failure or, at best, mediocrity.

2. what are the sources of topics and material for an essay?

The sources of topics and materials are as limited as the writer's interests and his willingness and ability to observe.

There are three basic sources or methods of gathering information and ideas. They are:

Direct experiences, things a writer was or is personally involved in; for example, an essay on ballet by someone who actually studied and performed ballet.

Here is an essay based on the direct experience of the writer.

Starting a New Life

It was May 16, 1979 and we were ready to leave the Philippines to go to the United States.

My sisters were crying then my eyes closed and thought for a minute. I didn't know if I still wanted to leave.

We went in the car very slowly. I looked at our house and smiled. We passed our school and places that helped us learn and grow up. We went in the airplane and read all the letters from my friends and relatives. Some made me laugh and some made me cry. I didn't know if I wanted to cry because I left my family, or to smile because I was going to see my parents.

Today, I think of the past, but I'm happy.

Carmita J. Cruz

Personal observation, things a writer has personally observed, even though she wasn't actively involved; for example, someone who has observed others study and perform ballet.

Information from others, relying on information from other sources, not from personal active involvement or observation; for example, reading ballet books, seeing ballet films, listen to others talk about ballet.

A topic for an essay can spring from any of these basic sources; in addition, a well-researched essay could conceivably involve all three sources.

3. how to limit the topic and the burden of research

There are a few things for a writer to consider before finally selecting a topic on which to write. The fact that it has relevance and meaning to him and that he has a real purpose for writing about the topic is paramount, but there are some other points of which one must be aware:

limiting the topic A writer may decide, "I want to do a 500-word expository essay on the history of the human race." This is certainly a noble enterprise; however, it might be better to cut down on the size of the topic (to, at least, the history of the human race since 3000 B.C. or the history of the American Indian living in southern New York State).

the burden of research   The writer should be aware of the potential difficulty in researching the topic. There are basically two things to consider:

How available and plentiful is information on the topic? Abraham Lincoln's presidency should not be a problem in researching and getting the needed information; numerous books, articles, and experts on Lincoln exist and can easily be found and used. What it's like to ride a bicycle around the world may prove a more difficult topic to research, though possible.

What will be the primary source of information? The writer should consider how to research the topic best (through direct experience, personal observation, or information from others), and understand the personal commitment of time, effort, and energy the research would entail. For example, George Plimpton decided that the best way to research certain sports was to actually participate with top professionals in that sport. He played quarterback for a National Football League team and boxed with a champion; others have observed sports as spectators and interviewed athletes but never actively involved themselves in the sport; still others did their main research by reading books and articles and interviewing sports personalities.

What is the writer's purpose of writing about the topic? There are numerous reasons for writing about a topic: to present known data; to communicate the writer's unique viewpoints; to motivate the reader to action; to create an emotional response from the reader; to convince a reader of a certain belief or attitude.

The writer needs a clear understanding of her purpose because the development and presentation of material in the essay will depend on that purpose. If she wants to convince someone to do something, for example, she would use the argumentative essay style.

4. who is the intended audience for the essay?

The depth of research and what should be covered and discussed in the essay would depend on the audience for whom the essay is intended. The more sophisticated (knowledgeable and experienced) the audience, the more involved and detailed the essay would have to be.

A six-year-old would probably have little interest in knowing that a cheetah is scientifically called "acinonyx jubatas," but he would like to know it's the fastest animal on earth.

Another point to consider is how receptive the audience would be to the topic and presentation of the essay. The writer should know the likely audience of her essay and predict what new information or ideas, or old information and ideas presented in a unique way, would be of interest and concern to the intended readers.

The writer might want to slant how and what she writes to the public she is trying to reach. Diction can vary—for one audience, "I have a strong craving for caviar" might be best, for another, "I have a Jones for pizza" might communicate better. Examples used to illustrate a point can vary—in writing about heroes for a ten-year-old child, it might be better to use a well-known current figure as an example than some obscure figure who lived 350 years ago.

The thing I look for more than anything else when reading the essays of young writers is the commitment to communicating their truths, feelings and beliefs to the intended audience.

5. what to write about the selected topic

Importance of Encouragement

Remember when you were young and everybody was winning different trophies and awards—If you didn't win the thing you were trying to win you felt down.

Your parents or friends usually encouraged you to try again and you kept trying and trying until you won. Do you remember now? My mom probably could.

When you have a child you should *encourage* him to read, write, race, draw, behave, etc. This will help your child very, very much because he or she will believe in you and will think that you want him to try a little of everything until he finds what he does best and improve it.

Your child/children need your encouragement so that they will try extra hard so they can come home and say, "Mommy (Daddy), I won!" This will make both of you feel very happy.

If you love your child/children you should encourage him. It will mean alot to him.

For ex. Child: "Mom, can I be in the race?"
         Mom: "Sure, but try hard."

Tell your child to try very hard.

Beth Wallace

In this essay, Beth, a fifth-grader, *knew* what she wanted to say and stress.

She presented the way she understands and observes some aspect of existence (what happens if encouragement is given to a child).

She touched on how things are interrelated (how encouragement relates to leading a happier life).

She made a prediction (a parent who gives encouragement will receive benefits as well as the child).

She discussed her personal viewpoint (the importance and positive effects of encouragement).

The writer should be aware, *before* starting to write an essay, of what she is trying to convey to the reader and what effect she is trying to have on the reader. She could include in her essay a presentation of what factually exists in this world; an emphasis on the relationship and interdependence of people, places, things, activities, and experiences; an explanation that helps readers understand why things are as they are; an indication of the future direction of things; a statement of a subjective point of view about the topic; a creative-imaginative statement that is based on truth but goes beyond to help convey a writer's personal reality to others.

The writer can begin (or extend) his research when he knows the direction in which he is heading—he has chosen his topic as specifically and precisely as necessary, knows what and who the audience will be, and understands what he would like to convey to that audience.

When all the material has been researched, he is ready to write.

how to write the essay

Samuel Johnson has described the essay as "A loose sally of the mind; an irregular indigested piece, not a regular orderly composition."

I suspect Mr. Johnson read some poorly written essays.

If anything, the essay should be based on careful consideration, research, and observation of the topic, with facts and ideas presented in a clear, orderly, logical, and well-organized writing style. An essay should be a very digestible communication that helps expand the awareness and understanding of the reader.

elements of writing a successful essay

Read over your compositions and, when you meet a passage which you think is particularly fine, strike it out.

Samuel Johnson

I'll let you make your own judgment about Samuel Johnson's advice. What I will present are some of the essential factors which can help determine how successfully an essay has been written and how well it communicates to others and creates the effects the writer intended.

Read the following essay on brotherhood, entitled, "Walk Together, Work Together." It was written by Ann Arthur, a junior-high-school student. After you read it, consider whether it was a successfully written essay. List why you think it was or wasn't. Then after reading the following section, re-read the essay and again consider whether it was successfully written.

Walk Together, Work Together

Yesteryear holds a cluster of unsuspected terrorist acts, wars, riots and genocides to fill our minds forever. For each breath we take is placing a cold clamp on the space dominated by human beings. Seldom do we catch a phrase that fills our body with an undescribable warmth and a surge of goodwill.

Reaching out to those around us has always been one major problem for man. Since the beginning of time itself, we have frantically struggled to develop a system of communication. Now that this system is only slightly beyond what we call perfection, another obstacle blocks the path of relating to one another. We must determine for ourselves whether we feel that the need for understanding each other is greater than the need for communication. If a single grunt could symbolize "I love you" the scholars of the world would abandon their entire language collection and begin investing in the uses of this priceless grunt.

For centuries so-called material things have come to replace what we as a group lack. Precious are the things that last, those we can add to and build a future upon, rather than material things that eventually fade away.

I'm not stating that the human race is doomed forever. We have come a long way and we have made many giant steps toward equality, friendliness, and respectfullness for everyone. Remember that although we have managed to ignite the candle, its wax touches everyone. Not evenyone wishes to be burned and a swift wind can dim the light that glowed for years.

In determining whether an essay has been successfully written, consider the following points:

1. *Does the essay communicate a central theme, idea, purpose?*

After reading the essay, can you clearly understand what the writer wanted to communicate? Do you understand what the writer was intending to do with the essay she wrote?

2. *Does the writer stick to the subject?*

Writing is easy: All you do is sit staring at a blank sheet of paper until the drops of blood form on your forehead.

Gene Fowler

Perhaps it's these drops of blood which interfere with the clarity of thought, leading so many writers to meander around, forgetting the concept, idea, or information they are trying to communicate.

I remember one student, Debbie, a very bright, self-motivated student (self-driven might describe her better) who *had* to excel. She had the impression that more was better and would write very extensive and wordy compositions, far beyond what was necessary. Invariably, Debbie would take a topic like "The Life Cycle of a Snail" and go off on a tangent and write about irrelevant things like the best escargot recipes in the French restaurants of Omaha, Nebraska.

Two things finally worked to help Debbie stick to the subject: a half-serious threat to have her write fifty times everything she unnecessarily added, and having her rate what she was writing on the following scale:

Necessary for understanding the topic -	2 points
Helpful to understanding the topic -	1 point
Neither necessary nor helpful to understanding the topic -	0 points

3. *Does the writer clearly develop and present ideas and information?*

Robert Louis Stevenson wrote, "Don't merely write to be understood. Write so that you cannot possibly be misunderstood."

development Writing so as not to be misunderstood should reflect in the way the writer develops and presents his material. Development of a topic involves how the writer organizes or arranges the written material. The logical, systematic, and orderly presentation of material makes an essay easier to read and understand. The writer should create a flow of information and ideas that leads the reader to a full awareness and understanding of what the writer is trying to communicate.

The writer has to decide how to develop the topic. For example:

a) Chronological time sequence—The essay follows the order of what happened first, second, third.

b) Simple to complex—The writer first presents the easily understood or agreed upon facts or concepts, leading to the more difficult ones.

c) Most important to least important material—This is the pattern of a newspaper story, which presents the most important information first, leaving the less critical data for the end.

d) Least important to most important material—This is a way of building to a climax, helping to maintain the involvement of the reader.

e) From specifics to generalizations (inductive)—The writer presents specific facts, ideas, and observations, then draws a conclusion (generalization) based on them.

The following essay will illustrate the inductive arrangement of material:

> I found out how lovely it is to write. I like to do the wanted posters because I felt I was talking to Mr. Percy. I got new ideas and did a lot of things that were fun. *I liked being in the workshop.*

6. From generalization to specifics (deductive)—The writer presents a basic viewpoint (generalization or conclusion) and leads from that to specific facts, ideas, and observations. Here's a sample deductive essay:

> *I liked being part of the creative writing workshop.* I liked all the creative things we did even though sometimes I could not think so fast. I really enjoyed the Haiku's, the stories, the roses are red, it was really fun. Another thing I like about the workshop is that I could get away from classroom.

7. From cause to effect—The writer first discusses causes and then the resulting effects.

presentation   To present the material of an essay, a writer should consider several things, but most importantly she must not assume that the reader knows what she (the writer) knows and understands. There's a play on the word assume which is appropriate: when you assume, it makes an *ass* (of) *u* (and) *me*. The concept of not assuming the reader knows what the writer knows relates to the viewpoint of writing so as not to be misunderstood.

The writer must decide how to present the material. For example:

By using details and examples—A writer will communicate more successfully when she uses concrete and realistic details and examples to explain and expand on abstract concepts and information.

By defining key terms—I recently had the confusing experience of reading an expository essay on how to use a camera my wife bought. To someone familiar with cameras and photography, I'm sure the following would be easy to understand; to me, it was baffling.

> For each f/stop up, the light is reduced one half. Accordingly when the aperture is increased by one f/stop, the exposure is doubled and when it is increased by two f/stops the exposure is quadrupled.

I had to look up the definitions for "aperture" (the size of the opening in a lens), "f/stop" (when referring to a number preceded by f/ it means the aperture is being spoken about), and "exposure" (the amount of light hitting the film) before I could understand the essay's point.

When I understood the definitions of those three terms and read that the lower the f/stop number, the larger the lens opening—f/1.4 has a much larger lens opening, allowing in more light, than f/16—I finally understood what the essay was saying when it mentions, "When the aperture is increased by one f/stop."

If the writer had only written for the likely audience who would read her essay, she would *not* have assumed as much as she did, causing as much confusion as she did (luckily, I knew the importance of looking up words I didn't understand).

I can't stress strongly enough that the writer must know her intended audience and present her material according to the depth of awareness and understanding likely readers will bring with them.

Style—The combination of distinctive features of writing that reflects the writer's personality and character.

Samuel Johnson has written, "Your manuscript is both good and original; but the part that is good is not original, and the part that is original is not good."

The degree to which a writer has developed his own style adds to the originality of the essay he has written; how good his work is will be reflected in the eyes of the reader, especially one who knows and appreciates the effort and growth of the writer.

It is important to encourage and acknowledge the writer's efforts and experimentation at finding his unique style of writing.

Here are two statements that characterize different styles of writing about the same subject:

> Parents should not embarrass their child, they should not call them stupid, bighead, skinny or other names that might embarrass them in front of their child's friends or in public.

Ann[1]

[1]Percy, p. 52.

Don't correct or embarrass kids in front of other people. It messes up pride.

Linden[2]

Style involves the ways in which a writer puts down the words she has chosen to use. Things to consider are:

tone   The writer may decide to be serious, humorous, sarcastic, cynical, straightforward, imaginative, sophisticated, down to earth.

diction   The choice and use of words by the writer; when Linden wrote, "It messes up pride," the use of the word "messes" is an example of his diction.

Another student, Reggie, wrote about punishment. He began, "Dig yourself beat on my head; dig yourself my clothes are all red." "Dig yourself" is an expression, a part of the diction that is unique to Reggie's style of writing.

Diction can be varied in several ways and involves numerous choices and decisions by the writer. Some choices involving diction include formal standard English ("greetings") or slang, street language ("what's up?"); polysyllabic ("supplicate") or monosyllabic ("pray"); abstract words ("masculinity," "femininity") or concrete words ("man," "woman"); general words ("the money") or specific ("$329 dollars"); should words be constantly repeated throughout what's written or should synonyms be used; which colorful and descriptive words should be used.

Mark Twain wrote, "The difference between the right word and the almost right word is the difference between lightning and lightning bug."

Part of the creative process in writing essays centers on the diction of the writer. Allow the writer leeway in her choice and use of words; encourage her invention and experimentation with words. Stress the use of the *diction*ary, thesaurus, or any other helpful material or tool.

preciseness and conciseness of the writing   Preciseness refers to how definite and exact the writing is; conciseness refers to how

[2]Percy, p. 53.

quickly and succinctly the writer expresses himself. Things to be aware of:

Are sentences long or short, simple or complicated? Generally, shorter sentences are simpler and easier to understand.

How many words are used? Is there a luxuriant elegance and abundance of words—if so, how many are unnecessary—or is there a paucity of verbiage—if so, would more verbosity help enhance the aesthetic and practical qualities of communication evidenced in the lucubrations of the essayist?

How did you like the style of my last paragraph? Whatever your response, I ENJOYED WRITING IT THAT WAY. I guess I could have said—too many words? How many unneeded? Too few words? How many needed? But, *I enjoyed* the luxuriant elegance and abundance of words used.

grammatical correctness and consistency of the writing   When the writer's grammatical incorrectness interferes with the reader's understanding and enjoyment of what's being communicated, it must be corrected; for example, "Yesterday we will want to, if you ask me, work with us."

I must admit that what concerns me is not so much the grammatical correctness of a child's writing, but how well it communicates. I do not negate the need and importance of understanding and using correct grammar, but when working with young writers on creative writing, my stress is on their enjoyment, involvement, and satisfaction for communicating what they want, in the way they want.

Re-read Ann's essay, using the following basic considerations for evaluating an essay (this list is a good guide for students to use when evaluating their essays):

1. Do you understand the basic theme of the essay?

2. Do you understand the writer's purpose for writing the essay?

3. Does the writer stick to the subject?

4. Does the writer clearly develop the subject? How did she organize (arrange) the material she wrote about?

5. How effective was the presentation? Was there a good use of specifics and examples, such as quotes, anecdotes, and sample illustrations; did the writer *not* assume too much about the audience; how effective was her style of presentation (consider the tone of the writing; diction; preciseness and conciseness; correct grammar)?

some helpful suggestions
for writing a composition

Topics reside in the mind, spirit and environment of everyone. Cam Solari, educator and writer, said, "Kids are dammed up with thoughts, concepts and awarenesses. . . ."

Part of helping a student find a topic is helping him feel safe and secure enough to communicate those dammed up thoughts, concepts, and awarenesses. If you sincerely value, accept, and acknowledge the truths, beliefs, and attitudes of a young writer, you've set the stage for the writing of essays.

A key factor in a writer's finding a topic to write about is her ability to observe and experience her environment. There are an infinite number of activities that can help a writer develop this ability.

One interesting activity is to ask students to find things they never observed in an environment with which they are familiar—their bedroom, the classroom.

Another successful activity I've used to help students observe their environment is based on a character in Robert Heinlein's *Stranger in a Strange Land,* the Fair Witness. A Fair Witness can not tell a lie and can only tell what she has actually observed; she can never infer or guess or have an opinion; she only deals in facts. I ask students to tell me the color of a piece of paper; they only see one side, which is black, while the other, unseen side is blue. Invariably the observers say the paper is black. I then discuss the concept of a Fair Witness, and how a Fair Witness would say, "The side that I see is black"; she would not assume that the other side was the same color without having actually seen the other side. I stress that a Fair Witness assumes nothing.

I then have a student stand, and I ask the class to describe her from the point of view of a Fair Witness. I deliberately pick a girl with hair covering her ears, and at some point I ask, "How many ears does she have?" Invariably the answer is two. I ask, "How do you know? Remember a Fair Witness only knows what he actually observed for himself." I reinforce this idea in several ways (if you're adventurous, you can ask whether she is a boy or a girl and stress, "How do you know? How would a Fair Witness know?" You could send a student to observe another class and come back and discuss what she has observed. Correct anything she says that involves an assumption or inference—an observation that the class was empty, based on looking through a window in a closed door, should be followed by the question, "How do you know no one was hiding in the closet?"

Literature of all kinds abounds with material that can spark ideas for the writer. Encourage and actively help a student to read, read, read. Literature is a wonderful tool for the young essay writer, as well as the person working with him. Literature is not only a wealthy source of ideas; it also helps students learn about things through indirect experience; it can help students learn how to write better by observing how established writers present and develop ideas and information; it can motivate students to write.

An activity to help open up a student's flow of ideas for topics is to have him invent topics and think about them as possible essay topics—how they can be developed, what the purpose would be.

I firmly believe that a student will not lack topics on which to think, discuss, and write if she is allowed to observe, explore, and experience her environment and all that resides within it; if she feels safe and secure enough to express her feelings, thoughts, beliefs, and knowledge, knowing that what she says will be valued and accepted (not necessarily agreed with, but accepted without invalidation).

writing the composition

how to start   A good beginning should get the reader's attention, involvement, and interest in the essay, as well as indicate the theme and purpose of the essay.

Some possible ways to open an essay are:

Begin with a relevant quote.

Use a creative and inventive title (which can be repeated at the start of the essay) that tells what the essay is about.

Start with an anecdote relevant to the topic.

State your conclusion, especially if it's a novel or controversial one.

Use something unexpected or different, like an unusual word or expression.

State what you hope the reader will gain as a result of reading the essay; for example, a better understanding of the topic or the motivation to work for or against something.

the middle   Writing the middle of an essay essentially involves being aware that the development and presentation of the material is relevant and effectively communicates what is intended.

Rudyard Kipling wrote something to keep in mind:

> I keep six honest serving men
> (They taught me all I knew):
> Their names are *what* and *why* and *when,*
> And *how* and *where* and *who*.

The middle should especially serve those men.

the ending   When the intended communication and the effect to be created on the reader has been delivered, *end*! The ending can vary depending on the purpose of the essay. You can end with a question (if the intention was to heighten the reader's awareness); summarize (if the purpose was to present data and viewpoints); suggest things to do (if the purpose was to motivate action).

Help the reader know and feel the composition has ended by use of an anecdote, quote, statement, or whatever is appropriate. It's important that the reader feels there is no reason for the writer to have written any more.

what it all means,
or, my perfect lesson

Given all the previous information and viewpoints on the essay, what does it mean in terms of actively helping students develop their interest and skill in writing essays?

I would like to answer, and explain, by sharing "my perfect lesson."

I'm sure we can all reflect on those things or times in our lives when we successfully attained a personal goal, knowing there was no way to improve the activity or get a better result. It might be fun to take a moment and remember one or more such instances in your life.

January 17, 1969, was a cold, wintry day in Brooklyn, New York. There were dark clouds crossing the sky and the cold wind was pushing against the windows, trying to visit our classroom. My class and I felt the excitement that comes with the anticipation of a soon-to-arrive heavy snowfall.

I closed the lights in our room and played the recording of "Winter" from Vivaldi's "The Four Seasons" (I "just" happened to have the record in class). I then turned on the blue fluorescent light in our newly cleaned goldfish tank; the bottom was covered with blue gravel and several pieces of coral.

I asked my fifth-graders to observe the movement and shapes of the clouds racing across the sky and to "feel" the trees blowing in the wind. I suggested they watch the multicolored fish in the tank while listening to Vivaldi's music. I insisted there be no talking and asked them to reflect in their own ways, and in their own personal environments, on what peace is. When they felt ready, they were to write an essay entitled, "Peace Is."

Every one of the thirty-two children in my class became *totally* involved in that activity—*every one.*

After several minutes they began writing; no one spoke or interrupted anyone's train of thought. There was a very special feeling in the class, an awareness that each individual was in touch with deeply personal truths, emotions, and experiences.

The tone and flow of creation lasted for one hour. When they had completed their writing, the children quietly brought me their first drafts, then very calmly and gently left the room.

I stayed at school late that day and read their essays. Tears actually began to flow, the beauty and feeling of each child's essay touched me more deeply than anything I had ever created with that class. The warmth, calmness, and thoughtfulness of the essays reflected the childrens' sincere efforts at communicating their truths, experiences, viewpoints, and feelings about peace.

I would like to share some first drafts with you:

Thoughts of Peace

Peace Is. . . .

Kittens sleeping softly in a box of softness, Peace is not war. Peace is fish, gerbils and hamsters and other animals not being afraid of being harmed. Sitting on a iceberg, floating in the ocean. Rolling and lying calm on soft green grass. Peace is sitting and writing little poems. Sleeping and dreaming of soft pretty quiet dream. To contemplate is to be in peace. Peace is to be loved by many. To play in a peaceful way is peace. Peace is to give and not to receive. Those are my ideas of peace.

Susan

Peace

Peace is to me calmness, tranquility, love and beauty. Relaxation and the feeling of running through a sheet of grass on a hot summer's day. It feels so refreshing and calm. Goldfish swimming in such a graceful manner. Peace is soft music putting you to sleep. Peace is calmness that you have over violence, and love over taking your heart. Peace is reunions of the families. A child with out a mother to love and finally finding someone who will love and protect you as long as you live.

Laurae

Peace is:

Everything quiet and daydreaming. Peace is having not a worry in the world. For there to be soft music. Peace makes you think of being on a stage doing ballet. Peace is when you feel like you're about to go to sleep. Peace is being under a tree watching the sun waving. Peace is like walking around knowing you are not going to be harmed. And to cuddle up with an animal by the fireplace, when it is cold outside. Peace is waking up in the morning watching the dawn.

Javette

I made a point of personally discussing the students' creations individually with them and asked if they would like to share their work with others (they all agreed). I asked them to proofread (edit) their essays, discussing some general things to look for—mechanical errors (spelling, punctuation); any changes in the wording to better communicate their feelings and truths. The final drafts were totally their creations. I displayed every child's essay and used excerpts from each essay for our class magazine.

The pattern of this essay-writing activity is one you can follow with your students:

Stimulate their interest in and get their agreement to writing on some topic.

Allow them to reflect (and research as needed) on that topic.

Have them write about the topic.

Discuss their writing with them.

Allow them to change their essay as they feel is needed.

Share their final draft with others (if the writer agrees).

I would like to close with the hope that an increased understanding of the essay will lead to your helping young writers use this invaluable tool for self-expression, discovery and communication.

six

poetry

6 O'Clock

6 O'clock in the morning—
      in my morning,
The sun is mellow
The breeze is cool
My bed gives security
My mind drifts where it may,

6 O'clock in the morning—
      in my morning,
And I feel dreamy as I
look out my window with half-closed eyes
The sheet on my body is
refreshing
And I slowly move my feet back
and forth
under the spread at the foot of my bed
My sister is asleep—she's
not really there
My room seems to be bare.

6 O'clock in the morning—
    in my morning,
The little brown sparrow can be seen
on the twig
He's chirping, the bees are
hovering near
The grass is green as
emeralds
and the leaves are rich and full
And it's nice to lay here and
take it all in . . .

    But the sun is now getting
Brighter
And the cool nice breeze has ceased
My sister's tossing and turning
and my sheets are getting hot
My thoughts are turning
evil
My mouth has a bitter
taste
The sparrow is fighting with
another
And it's 6 O'clock in
the *morning.*

Siobhan

Poetry became a strong and beautiful way to make a statement on something. I found it challenging and emotional. I could be clever and relay a message, a thought. Mostly feelings. It let me take something from within and give it a voice, so that others could read it "from without," and hopefully, enjoyably, feel it within.

The writing was truly original. I took it only from the life I experienced.

. . . I felt my poetry was a message from me, and from many others also, to many, many more.

The above quote was taken from a letter written to me by Siobhan

Gamble, whose poetry, including the poem at the beginning of the chapter, has been featured throughout the book.

To Siobhan, the writing, understanding, and ease of poetic expression and creation is as natural and instinctive as breathing; it's as if she had been born with a personal poetic Muse resting on her shoulder. When I worked with Siobhan I realized she knew and understood what poetry is far better than I, and my role was to *avoid* suppressing and inhibiting her creativity while giving her whatever encouragement, validation, and direction she needed.

two goals

The poetic talent and interest possessed by Siobhan are, unfortunately, the exception rather than the rule. There are two major goals for teaching and involving students in writing poetry; they are 1) to help students develop an insightful, sensitive, and understanding poetic eye, and 2) to help them develop the ability to aesthetically express their thoughts, feelings, and awarenesses through poetry.

what is poetry?

The question probably invites as many answers as there are poets and readers of poetry.

Carl Sandburg has written, "This question no man has ever answered in such a way that all men have said, 'Yes, now we know what poetry is.' What is poetry for one person may be balderdash or hogwash for another."

Take a moment to reflect and answer for yourself the question, what is poetry?

a thoughtfelt thing

Perhaps the best way to discuss poetry is not to define what it is, but describe it.

Robert Frost has described poetry as being " . . . a thoughtfelt thing"; indeed, a poem's beginnings emanate with a thought, an idea, that the poet feels and needs or wishes to express through poetry. That poetic expression has a feeling of language that separates it from prose writing; its rhythm and sound, its flow and choice of words, the images it creates in the reader's eye, the emotions it touches and reveals, all help create the poetic impact.

A poem is felt as much as it is read, and it is when a student feels poetry that he will truly begin to write poetry. The truth is, in order to actively involve a student in the writing of poetry, you must help him feel it.

Until recently—in fact, until preparing this chapter for the book—I never realized how turned off I became to both the reading and writing of poetry as a result of how poetry was taught to me. Basically, with but one exception, my teachers did not try to help me feel poetry; their concern was that I analyze it for such technical things as rhyming patterns, the precise way certain words helped create a specific mood, symbols used, and meter.

help a potential poet develop a positive feeling for poetry

To involve a student in the writing of poetry, help him *feel* the mental, emotional, and spiritual effects it creates on him, and understand the personal awareness and insights that develop from having read a poem. If you help a student develop a positive feeling for and about poetry, the technical understanding will come later.

There are three basic ways to help a potential poet develop this positive feel for poetry. You must:

Have, and communicate, a positive feeling for poetry.

Read poetry to your students.

Provide opportunities and experiences to develop the tools of a poet.

communicate your positive feel for poetry

I have been fortunate enough to have had one truly inspirational teacher in all my years of schooling. She taught a college course in classical literature. Miss Lachman was a delicate woman in her late fifties who would sit on her desk, reading excerpts from one of our required readings for the week. Her joy, love, and passion for these works of classical writing were infectious. Tears would well up in her eyes when she read a particularly moving and beautifully written passage.

I found myself very moved by her sincerity of feeling. (A teacher's tears can be very touching and affecting.) I had taken the course reluctantly (it was a requirement for graduation), yet Miss Lachman, much to my amazement, helped me feel and appreciate, to a much greater depth than I ever could have imagined, the importance and beauty of the works we studied.

Personally, I've always had a special feel and appreciation for humorous and tell-it-like-it-is poetry; I tend not to enjoy or appreciate dark, forbidding, and deeply symbolic poetry.

My students' poetic creations tended to reflect my feelings; they picked up on my enthusiasm.

You must find those poetic forms for which you have a sincerity of feeling. Those are the ones to present and with which you should help involve your students. If you attempt to teach poetry out of obligation, with little personal interest and involvement, you will tend to have students who create out of obligation, with little personal interest and involvement, or who will be turned off to poetry.

read poetry to your students

Puppy Dog

Puppy Dog, Puppy Dog, run at my heels,
Chase the leaves, hear the wind
See how it feels. Roll over, lay down,
Beg, sit, stay. Puppy Dog,
Puppy Dog, you must obey.
Be lovable, Be faithful, Be kind to me,
Puppy Dog, Puppy Dog, I'll always love
Thee.

Siobhan

Siobhan wrote this poem when she was in fourth grade. It is one of a collection of her early poetry that I used to read to my classes.

Siobhan's poems were one of the best tools I had to involve my students in poetry. I realized that perhaps the most important thing I could do to interest my students in writing poetry was to read poems specifically selected for them. My selection was determined by the students' interest, maturity, and sophistication, and by *my* personal tastes, preferences, and interests.

Siobhan's writing skill never ceased to amaze and inspire many of my students, especially when I told them she was ten years old when she wrote much of what I read.

By hearing poetry, students can develop a feel for certain forms and styles of poetic expression. Knowing about a poetic form, and feeling good about it because of previous experience with it (from your reading), will help motivate students to use that form of creative expression when their poetic Muses rests on their shoulders.

Understand that students will be turned off by inappropriate poems or a teacher's poor reading of very appropriate poetry (a bland, monotonal reading that conveys all the joy, warmth, or feeling of a puddle of slush). Rehearse before you read, and communicate the rhythm, meaning, and feel that the writer intends. Use the punctuation marks, word groupings, and stresses that the writer has used. Perform the poem, don't just read it.

Basically, if you don't feel a poem, *don't* read it!

Writing and sharing *your* poems can be very helpful in developing your students' feel and interest for poetry.

I used to create and share personal poems for students in my classes. For example,

> *Roses are red*
> *Clouds are white*
> *Linden Jackson*
> *Is outta sight!*

This led to a flood of "roses-are-red" poetry.

> *There is a boy whose name is Lou.*
> *He loved to be with you-know-who.*
> *He kissed her nose,*
> *Stepped on her toes,*
> *And on his shin he felt her shoe.*

Needless to say, that limerick provoked quite a response from, and for, Lou. There was also a great deal of guessing about who "you-know-who" was. Limericks became a favorite poetic writing form for that class.

Finding an appropriate point in the day for reading a relevant poem is another helpful thing to do. For example, after the class has been somewhat noisy, you can recite the following:

> *A wise old owl lived in an oak,*
> *The more he saw, the less he spoke.*
> *The less he spoke, the more he heard.*
> *Why can't we all be like that bird?*

provide opportunities
for experiencing and developing
the tools of a poet

A poet has several tools that he uses: the ability to observe, perceive, and experience his environment; the ability to appreciate and draw ideas from those "thoughtfelt" things he finds in his environment; the creative imagination to see a direction in which he wants to "travel" with that idea; the awareness and understanding of various poetic forms he could use to express his idea; a working knowledge of words and the language of poets (similes, metaphors, rhythmic flow, imagery).

Take the time to introduce, develop, and enhance the basic tools of a poet. Do it in a way that validates, or helps him expand his ability to perceive and create poetry.

Help the writer use his five senses to observe his environment—taking walking trips through a garden while blindfolded; studying a particular object, like an apple, observing all that can be sensed; watching people; listening to birds; smelling the grass; tasting some food; feeling the morning dew; trying to see what is happening behind while looking straight ahead. Heighten, in whatever way you can, the poet's interest and ability to observe and perceive.

Give and create opportunities to use the writer's imagination—brainstorm ideas for poems about some object in the environment; think in completely nonsensical ways about how to use words and ideas (a story of a pickled, banana-fudge-topped sirloin steak); decide what the clouds say when they look down at the people on earth. Help the writer break whatever chains limit his imaginative reach.

Play with words, study words, use words, think words. There are numerous activities to help develop a child's speaking and writing vocabulary and his understanding and appreciation for words. For example, keep word files of unusual words; use new words heard in poetry or found in a book to describe experiences; use specific words to describe an event (The girl walked to the car: what kind of girl—skinny, silly, wild, girl with pigtails; how did she walk—with a slight limp, a shuffle, a hop in her step; what was the car like—old, rusted, shiny, a limousine).

When appropriate—when the students have an interest in form and have the maturity and sophistication to understand and create with various forms—introduce poetic forms like the limerick, couplet, haiku. Help students understand the specific technical requirements as they relate to a poetic form. For example, tell them that the couplet is two successive lines that rhyme and have the same rhythmic flow, such as:

The tree birds sing
To welcome spring.

The more familiarity a writer has with all the possible forms and styles of poetry, the greater his potential ability to create as a poet.

some characteristic elements
of the poetic craft

Until a student is really interested in poetic techniques, devices, and analysis, do not overbearingly teach them; do introduce elements of poetry appropriate to the learning and interest levels of the student and group. The more familiar you are with the craft of poetry, the better you will be able to involve your students in the writing of poetry.

Poetry has a rhythmic sound and flow, often referred to as meter. A poem's rhythm is influenced by the repetition of words, phrases, ideas, and silences, but the steady repeating pattern of stressed and unstressed syllables is what basically determines the rhythmic flow of a poem:

I sińg to yóu.

This is the common iambic rhythm of an unstressed syllable followed by a stressed syllable.

Poetry can *rhyme*. It's the sound of the word ending, not the letters, that determines rhyme. Be aware of forcing rhymes to fit the content of the poem or forcing the content of the poem to fit the rhyming words (very common among young writers):

> *I sit in my car*
> *Looking at a star*
> *Thinking of a bar*
> *From here it's far.*

Poetry uses language that creates distinctive word pictures to communicate experiences and ideas; it creates *images* of things (the way they look, feel, sound, and so on).

Poetry uses devices to help communicate what the poet intends. Robert Frost has written that a poet is successful "when he thinks of something in connection with something else that no one ever put with it before."

The following devices—tools—of a poet can help him communicate those connections:

similes   Using "like" or "as" to introduce comparisons of things: she runs like a cheetah; he looked like a concave lens.

metaphors   An indirect way to compare things, without using "like" or "as": Easter is glorious hats, painted eggs, and hopping rabbits; he is an iceberg under conditions of turmoil.

alliteration   Regular repetitions of consonant and/or vowel sounds: the big bad boy bit the bad banana; open to the only ode he wrote.

onomatopoeia   A word that sounds like the thing to which it refers: the *buzz* of the bee; the *hiss* of the snake.

personification   To give personal human qualities to inanimate objects: *the tree felt lonely*, standing by itself; *the clouds roared with anger* as they clashed together.

symbols   When what is written suggests more than the literal meaning of the words and phrases used:

> I Can Dream
>
> *A silver winged bird flies high*
> *   in the night*
> *His wings are studded with stars ever*
> *   so bright*
> *His call is like that from a delicate flute*
> *Played by the love of a maiden so true.*
> *My life cannot bring this sight to me—*
> *I can dream though—I*
> *   can dream.*
>
>   Siobhan

The "silver-winged bird" is a symbol.

imagery   Creating vivid descriptions and sensory pictures with words:

> Sleep is near me
>
> *His body and mine are gradually becoming unified,*
> *We will be one—*
>
> *We fight—my lids struggle*
> *with the weight of him*
> *My mind is confused and darkly blurred*
> *They close—he has won this round*
> *I force them open—I win this time*
> *But he is powerful*
> *And beckons convincingly to me—*
> *in his hand he holds Mystery*
> *for me—come dream*
> *And after one last effort I*
> *give in and close my eyes*
> *Sleep has conquered me*
> *Until he is fought off by the cavalry—*
> *a shaking hand.*
>
>   Siobhan

The preceding poem abounds with imagery.

hyperbole   Exaggeration used as a figure of speech: I waited *forever*; she weighs a *ton*.

analogy   Showing how things usually thought of as being different have similarities: comparing John's style of running a marathon with the persistent struggle of an ant carrying food to its home.

The familiarity with and understanding of how to use these various poetic devices can greatly enhance the poet's ability to create the effects he intends.

some common poetic forms

There are many forms of poetry; some will have more appeal to a poet than others. When a poet is familiar with these forms, he can decide which one is best to communicate what he intends.

free verse   Unrhymed poetry with an irregular form, having a cadence (rhythmic flow) that can be marked off as free verse lines and having an emotional and subjective content. The theme of the poem and the way the poem is developed are limitless:

Tears

Are tears worthless—when you cry
    over silly things?
Are they sacred—no matter how they're
    brought about?
Are your tears filled with the bitter taste of
    anguish, pain, loneliness, joy, relief
Fear, anger? Are they sweet nothings?
    Are they the same no matter where they come from?
Are they just a waste?

    Why are there tears?

            To cry.

                                        Siobhan

couplet The simplest form of rhymed verse. It consists of two lines, each with approximately the same number of syllables, with rhyming end words:

> *The four-year-old flows her dancing body through the air,*
> *The audience marvels at her poetry of motion—and stare.*

quatrain A four-line stanza, generally with the second- and fourth-line end words rhyming:

Us Colored Folks

Us colored folks
Don't know a thing
All we's good for is
to work and sing
Stupid and ugly,
Stink and loud
I'm a colored folk
And I sure am proud

Siobhan

This poem is a double quatrain, with two four-line stanzas.

haiku A Japanese poem of three-line verses, having a total of seventeen syllables in a pattern of:

1st line—five syllables
2nd line—seven syllables
3rd line—five syllables.

Haiku expresses feelings, thoughts, descriptions about nature. It tries to capture and communicate one main thought, the essential quality, about some aspect of nature. It deals with contrast, comparison, and relationships. Its beauty of imagery and aesthetic flow of words help create its impact:

> *The sun is shining*
> *Its golden warmness fills me*

I'm a child of earth

Siobhan

tanka   Similar in intent and poetic style to the haiku, concentrating on nature, but its form is five lines, not three as in haiku, having a total of thirty-one syllables. The pattern is:

1st line—five syllables
2nd line—seven syllables
3rd line—five syllables
4th line—seven syllables
5th line—seven syllables.

For example:

> *I breath the clean air,*
> *It seems to cleanse my body,*
> *It refreshes me.*
> *What a glorious pleasure,*
> *To feel my body rejoice.*

senryu   A Japanese poem similar to haiku, concerned with human nature, but usually humorous and not necessarily in keeping with the syllable requirements of haiku:

> *I look in the mirror*
> *I am again slim and trim*
> *Then my eyes open.*

cinquain   A five-line poem with the following pattern:

1st line—one word (or two syllables) gives title;
2nd line—two words (or four syllables) describes title;
3rd line—three words (or six syllables) expresses action;
4th line—four words (or eight syllables) expresses a feeling;

5th line—one word (or two syllables) another word for the title.

> *Dancer*
> *graceful, artistic*
> *glides, spins, leaps*
> *joy, pride, exhilarate, tender*
> *Ballerina*

limerick   A popular form of nonsense verse. There are five lines. The rhyming pattern is 1-1-2-2-1, with three beats in lines 1, 2, and 5, and two beats in lines 3 and 4. In lines 1, 2, and 5, the stress is on the second, fifth, and eighth syllables.

Line 5 usually ends with humor or surprise. The poet can use crazy spellings and unusual twists and have a creative, imaginative ball:

> *I have a baby named Kali*
> *I love to sit her on my knee*
> *I kiss her nose*
> *Bite on her toes*
> *Until she waters over me*

diamente   A structured form of writing that has seven lines and contains a contrast (a comparison that shows a difference between things). Its pattern is:

1st line—a noun that names an object or thought

2nd line—two adjectives that describe the noun

3rd line—three participles (-ing or -ed words) that relate to the noun

4th line—four nouns, two referring to the noun in line 1, two referring to the noun in line 7

5th line—three participles that relate to the noun in line 7

6th line—two adjectives that describe the noun in line 7

7th line—a noun that names an object or thought that is the opposite of the noun in line 1

PLAYER
swift, agile
running, hustling, competing
pride, fulfillment, numbness, dissatisfaction
sitting, watching, bored
lazy, motionless
SPECTATOR

This can provide a wonderful activity for reviewing the parts of speech used in the poem.

It would also be helpful to have a thesaurus and a book of synonyms and antonyms available. Allow every student to approach the poem from the way that's best for them. Some may want to start with both nouns, others will want to find opposite adjectives and nouns that relate to the adjectives.

I would like to close with Siobhan's quote that began this chapter. "Poetry became a strong and beautiful way to make a statement on something. I found it challenging and emotional. I could be clever and relay a message, a thought. Mostly feelings. It let me take something from within and give it a voice, so that others could read it 'from without,' and hopefully, enjoyable, feel it within."

Create some time to take something from within and share it with others.

When was the last time *you* wrote any poetry?

seven

fiction: the short story

On Eternal Guilt

I went outside the small dark house in order to get a breath of fresh air. It had just been raining in the yard, and now the sun was starting to shine through the clouds. I really intended to reflect upon the last few days of my life, for they had been traumatic. As I set foot into the great outdoors I noticed a small shrub. A drop of water was hanging from a barren and sickly branch.

"Are you all right?" I asked shyly.

The drop only twinkled a little in the bright light. It was going to ignore me; simply taken in by its own predicament. No one could help. This small and innocent drop was destined to fall into the soil.

I stood up slowly. My knees ached. This small drop had just demonstrated that with a little confidence and coolness, it could avoid being reliant on outside help. It did not ask help from one who was just a mere subject that would pass in and out of its life, as a fly would pass in and out of a kitchen.

I tried to reason with it. I felt genuine concern for its well being.

Yet, there it hung. The crystal drop's perilous fate seemed to be approaching as the branch tried desperately to shake it off.

I continued to plead with the drop, however, only the brilliance of the sun shone through. I saw a clear and emotionless internal perspective. I had the feeling that the drop had lost hope and was willing to accept its fate and go to its eternal resting place—the soil.

Keep a stiff upper lip I told myself. Not I nor a hundred tiny rivulets of drops could save this small and innocent one. I really had mixed emotions, for I did not know whether to be angry with the drop for being so selfish and stubborn, in which case I should walk away, or feel compassion for it and wait it out till the end. The drop was affecting my insecurities.

The sun began to set and a slight wind began to rustle the leaves. The clouds began taking over the sky. It looked like rain.

I threw my hands up in desperation.

"Why!" I shouted.

I looked down at my crystal companion. It no longer shone like a star. The twinkle had gone out of it and was replaced by a dull gray hue. It looked sad—really sad. Any minute it would plummet into the soil.

"Why should I concern myself with this object that does not want my help?" I asked myself.

"It's in your nature," was my response.

With a sudden renewed interest, I bent down very close to the drop. The drop began to wiggle and then—it died. I thought I heard a faint cough. I watched the tiny drop fall to its death, completely helpless. I was frozen in my position.

I stood up quickly and became aware of the look of horror that was on my face. I glanced quickly around the yard. Very quietly, I recited a brief kaddish for my friend.

"There'll be others," I said.

I re-entered the house and poured myself a scotch. In trying to escape from the world of hysteria that caused such great anxiety, I was confronted with yet another tragic matter. After thinking about that afternoon, I began to feel as though it were my fault that the drop had fallen. I had bent down so quickly, the drop was literally blown from its perch. I gulped down the rest of the scotch. Guilt set in as quickly as heartburn does after eating Italian food.

I didn't sleep that night. I kept visualizing the death and my reaction. I went to the bathroom and splashed some cold water on my face. In the morning, I decided to call Dr. Fernzwick, my psychiatrist.

After I told him the story in his office, he said to me, "Mark, why do you think the drop requested no assistance? Because it was selfish? The drop simply recognized the value of being independent. For once, that drop was ready to live its own life, even if it meant death! Once a drop, always a drop until the last drip!"

He rambled on for a few moments and then began to laugh hysterically. He always did. Sixty dollars an hour and he laughs.

Roger Jubas (high school student)

fiction

Robert Frost wrote, "There is no art to writing but having something to say."

Fiction—writing that employs the imaginary characters, events, and setting created by the writer—is a wonderful outlet for students who have something to say or need to say something.

Faith Delatorre, who has used creative writing extensively with junior-high-school students, commented, "A value of writing that's most important is that it would help my students work out a lot of confusion through their creating characters and scenes. It's like a catharsis when they put emotion in the proper place and scene, an emotion that could only be expressed when hiding behind a character."

Linden Jackson, a former student of mine, wrote, "The thing I like most about it (writing) is that it allows me to use my 'third eye' to make a whole new dimension and put it down on paper. It gives me the opportunity to enhance my individuality."

Roger Jubas's story, *On Eternal Guilt,* is a fine example of how fictional writing can be used to say something the writer needs or wants to say.

ideas, the kindling for writing;
form, the skeleton of writing

Before writing an imaginative narrative (story), the student needs to choose two things: an idea about which he wishes to write, and the narrative form for expressing his idea.

ideas

The idea, or theme, is kindling to the fire of creation. Story ideas are as limitless as the writer's perception of what exists in his physical, mental, social, emotional, and spiritual environment. Ideas can spring from: stories read by, or read to, the writer; the way someone stands on a street corner; the study of the metamorphosis of the butterfly; a thought presented by the teacher; a zany personal mental creation; an argument with a parent.

The writer must, at some awareness level, have a personal radar that will go, "click, what an idea for a story!" His sense of wonder and interest in his world and the world of others, accompanied by an ability to observe and truly perceive that which exists and an environment in which it's safe and validating for him to explore, discover, and communicate, will cause that "click" to sound many times.

The teacher's role in helping a writer get that magical "click" must never be underestimated. The teacher's encouragement and acknowledgement of a student's efforts and the presentation of what, why, where, when, and how to observe and perceive is invaluable. A teacher's motivation and gentle kicks in the behind to help a student write and develop her talent will help that writer search and find ideas to write about.

I recently received a note from a former student that included the following statement: "I want to *thank you* for helping me keep my talent alive—actually for blowing a strong breath of life into my talent!"

Her search for ideas continues . . . . YEAH!

form

The narrative form is the skeleton on which the idea is developed and communicated. Exposure to the various kinds of narrative forms can help a writer choose on which skeleton to build.

short story Generally, a short story has few main characters (perhaps one or two); the action is organized and carried out in a brief period of time; attention is given to communicate a meaning or concept the writer feels is important. The writer can use the third-person viewpoint (they, he, she) or first-person viewpoint (I, me, we) to help present and organize the plot of a story.

94

The short story can be: *adventure* (a hazardous, unusual, or exciting plot with an uncertain ending); *mystery* (puzzling and unknown elements in the plot that arouse curiousity in the reader); *science fiction* (using imagination to draw on scientific knowledge and speculation for the plot, setting, characters, and theme); *life anecdotes* (stories that are based, or could come, from everyday life situations); *humorous* (a sense of fun and comedy); *tragedy* (dealing with a serious, gloomy theme with a tragic conclusion).

Here is a fine example of a short story written by an eighth grade student.

Homeboy

Chano Hernandez grew up on a side street in East Los Angeles. He was always surrounded by violence. His father beat his mother. His mother and father beat him and his sister. They were very poor with little to eat.

When Chano was 16, he joined the Cholos of East 20th Street gang. He wore a red bandana and carried a knife and gun.

One Wednesday night while he and the other Homeboys in his gang were cruising Van Nuys Boulevard, they met with their rival gang, the Vatos of South Los Angeles Street. Some harsh words passed and the next thing they knew both gangs were having an all out rumble.

Switch blade knives clicked, chains jingled, and fists flew.

The police arrived in less than a minute after the fight began. They fired their guns in the air and told everyone to freeze. The members of the two gangs (those that could still run) ran in all directions.

Chano escaped the police and their guns. There was only one thing that he couldn't escape from and that was himself. For he knew that he had killed a man . . . and for no good reason.

Brian McCarthy (12 years old)

fable   A fictitious story, often including and about animals or inanimate objects that speak and are personified; its purpose is to teach a moral (a principle or rule for right conduct and survival).

myth   A type of story that usually concerns gods, god-like heroes, or heroes who are bigger than life; its purpose is to try to explain some belief or natural event or phenomenon.

fairy tale   A story, usually for a child, about magical creatures (elves, fairies, dragons, witches), involving legendary deeds and romance.

folk tale   A tale or legend passed down from generation to generation among a people or group.

legend   An unverifiable story handed down by tradition from earlier times, and popularly accepted as historical; it denotes a fictitious story often concerned with a real person, place, or other subject, and sometimes involving the supernatural.

To help a student become familiar with these various story forms, a teacher can read selections to her, show filmstrip stories, find selections for her to read, discuss movies, or write and share a story with her.

One of my students wrote, "My crazy teacher used to tell us zany stories, which led me to the belief that fictional stories get the attention of the reader. I wrote some wild stories for my crazy teacher and I found whoever would end up reading them would like them somehow or another."

I can attest that his zaniness more than matched mine. He was obviously influenced by my affinity for "zany" stories.

I strongly suggest you select and present material for which you have a real affinity. Your pleasure and interest can and will be noticed by your students and will more likely motivate their writing than presentation of material out of some sense of obligation. Of course, if your students express interest in something you don't particularly enjoy, I would recommend that you present and share that form of writing as positively as possible.

the basic story elements

Ralph Waldo Emerson wrote, "Imagination is not a talent of some men, but is the health of every man."

The health of Orestes is evidence by the beginning a tale he wrote:

Erosinum

Erosinum was from the Tyrine tribe: a group of people who had somehow managed to appear on the planet that men call Nereus, in the outer reaches of Alpha Centauri. Now he was picking his way up the rocks to get to the top of the mesa, which looked like the bow of a sinking ship coming up from the earth. It was extremely hot, and his loin cloth was sticking to him with sweat, he didn't like that.

The great bird, at least that's what he thought it was, came very rarely in the year. Now, as Erosinum neared the top, it began its circling, monotonous glide upward, toward the bright sun which beamed its wrath upon the hot sands of the desert. Erosinum never bothered to notice that the bird appeared only when the sun did. He never put it together in his mind, it was too hard to.

To help bring the imaginative stirrings of a writer's mind to the reality of a well-crafted piece of writing requires an awareness and understanding of how to use the basic elements of story writing: theme, plot, characterization, setting, and style. These can be learned or known "instinctively."

The teacher's awareness and understanding of these basic elements is essential to helping enhance the story-writing ability of a student.

theme (idea)   The theme is the writer's sense of what main concept or viewpoint is presented in the story. The theme is reflected and contained in the other story elements.

What do you consider Roger's theme is in the story, "On Eternal Guilt"?

plot   The plot is the organization and presentation of the story's events and situations; it's the plan and design of a story.

There is a commonly used formula for plot development: a protagonist (the main character of the story) has a goal he wishes to attain, but there's a barrier(s) he has to overcome in trying to reach his goal. The plot is built around his actions and efforts to overcome the barrier(s) and the actions and efforts to stop his progress, until he either wins and attains his goal or loses and fails to reach it.

Those of you who have written stories know how plot ideas spring forth. Sometimes your theme helps you visualize the entire plot; at other times the characters you've developed dictate certain plot situations. At times the conflict within the story demands that certain events take place. A wisp of cloud in the sky may trigger a plot idea.

However it evolves, the plot creates dramatic action and helps the writer, in a meaningful and entertaining way, present the theme, present and develop the character(s), and establish the setting of the story.

Raymond Chandler offers an observation about determining a plot: "At least half the mystery novels published violate the law that the solution, once revealed, must seem inevitable." The inevitability and believability of the story line is essential for a well-crafted story.

Re-read Roger's story and observe how he has developed his plot.

characterization　　Orestes, who wrote about "Erosinum" on the previous page, commented, "I like creating characters that reflect on me or characters that do things that I would not normally attempt. I get tremendous enjoyment in putting them through challenges."

Characterization involves the presentation and development of a story character so he is as well-known and understood by the reader as the writer wishes him to be.

A character can be revealed by his own actions, an explanation by the narrator, the character's dialogue (a character's dialogue, what he says and how he speaks, should be consistent with who and what he is as developed in the story), the dialogues of others, how he reacts to others, and how others react to him. As the story progresses, a character can be shown to change (for better or worse), and more can be revealed about him—little idiosyncracies shown, events that motivate the various character traits presented.

Here are two brief examples to show how we learn about characters from what is written about them or their dialogues.

What impressions do you get about A.E. Houseman, the writer of the following quote, and the person about whom he is writing: "Nature, not content with denying him the ability to think, has endowed him with the ability to write."

What about the impressions created by this one: "A book is a mirror: if an ass peers into it, you can't expect an apostle to peer out."—Georg Christoph Lichtenberg (Does the writer's name create an impression as well?)

What do you know and understand about the main character in Roger's story? How has Roger revealed the personality of the main character?

setting   The setting is the locale and time period of a story. It is essentially the background in which the story takes place and provides the physical, social, emotional, mental, and/or spiritual environment(s) of the story. In describing the setting, the writer can be as detailed and elaborate as he is able and as is appropriate for the story.

Think how you would describe the setting you're now in as you read this page. What would you describe? What details would you include? How would you convey the feeling and tone of the environment?

Observe how Roger described and presented the setting of his story.

style   Observe how Roger uses language to: reveal himself, present the action and plot, develop the main character's personality, and suggest what the theme is.

One specific thing to look for is his use of verbs, as verbs can create a great difference in how effectively an idea, mood, or action is communicated:

He looked at her.

He stared at her.

He glared at her.

The mood conveyed by "glared" is quite different than that conveyed by "looked."

Verbs help create vivid descriptions of flow and movement, because they are the action words. Which creates a better picture and tells more?

He jumped over the fence.

He leaped over the fence.

He catapulted over the fence.

Please turn to page 67 for a more complete discussion of style.

how to develop a story

Burton Roscoe has written, "What no wife of a writer can understand is that a writer is working when he's staring out of the window."

The writing process may involve a writer's staring out of a window, walking through the littered streets of the city, listening to a Mozart concerto, or watching television. The approach to developing a story can vary from writer to writer and from story to story by the same writer.

One method used to create a story is by focusing on one or more elements of the story—theme, plot, characterization, and setting—and deciding how they can relate and interact with each other. For example, there may be two strong characters about which to write a story; those characters are the foundation of the story. The writer can then decide on a setting appropriate to them, with that setting suggesting a plot, and the plot or the nature of the characters suggesting a theme.

A story I recently wrote began with the theme. I then searched for, and found, plot ideas to communicate that theme; by finding the plot, the characters and the setting jumped out at me.

Another approach to writing a story would be for the writer to focus on the goal to be reached and to decide on the various barriers that might keep the character(s) from reaching the goal. (The writer could use any arrangement of goal, barrier, and character to develop his story; the writer could start with characters, then find the goal, and finally come up with the barriers; or start with the barriers.)

There is no right or wrong way to approach, develop, and write a story. What works best for a particular writer and a particular story is what is important.

Look at Roger's story. How do you think he might have approached its development?

evaluating the story

It is best to work with a student to help him develop his own method and criteria for evaluating his stories. How well he understands the craft of writing will determine how sophisticated and detailed his evaluation will be.

In general, there are two things of which to be aware:

100

1. Does the story communicate what is intended, creating the effects intended?

2. What should be added, deleted, changed, or left untouched?

Some specific things to look for:

1. Theme—Is it clearly understood by the writer? Does it communicate to the reader? Is it "worth" writing about?

2. Plot—Are the action and presentation of various situations relevant and believable in helping the main character(s) try to overcome barriers to attain the goal (or fail to attain the goal)?

3. Characterization—Are the characters as well-known and understood as needed by the story? Are the characters consistent in action and dialogue throughout the story? Are the characters revealed more through action and dialogue than explanation? Are the characters real and believable?

4. Setting—Does it fit the story mood? Does it create the appropriate physical, social, emotional, mental, or spiritual environment?

5. Style—Has the language used been specific, action-oriented, clear, and descriptive?

6. Does the story satisfy?

One of my students wrote, "I like to invent a sequence of events as they come to my mind and write them on paper. It makes me feel like I'm inventing something that someday would be on TV or on the big screen or read in front of a group of distinguished people."

By understanding the basics of crafting a story, you, the teacher of creative writing, will be in a better position to help your students invent stories that achieve their dreams and goals.

Help them read, read, read, and write, write, write, write, write, write, write. The craft of writing will improve as the quantity of writing a student willingly does increases.

Linden wrote, "When I write, I like to be understood, and if someone can't understand it or fails to take an interest in it, I get turned off."

Help prevent writer turn-off. Help a writer create and develop his craft so that his writing is understood and of interest to others; this is especially true in the writing of fiction.

eight

creative writing and other curriculum areas

Delicate Things Like

Butterfly breath,
Tears from a rose
Laughter from the sunshine
The flower of a grain of sand
Smidgen of a peacock feather
Soft glitter in your love's eye
Fiery finger touch
Hair on your front tooth
Dragonfly wings
Light of a firefly
Gentle curdle of a baby
Steady purring of a sleepy kitten
The eyelash of a gnat

Siobhan

"Sure, teach creative writing, and dance, and music, and art, and self-awareness, and human relations. *But what about reading, math, science, thinking and study skills, social studies, and grammar?* There is only so much time in the day. Creative writing and all that other stuff just has to wait until I have the time to fit it in." (A commonly heard complaint)

Having been in a classroom for fourteen years, I know and understand that viewpoint very well. There *is* a finite amount of time in the day. I found I was always making decisions on what to teach and include in my educational program—that is, what activity would make the most important contribution to my students' success in school and best help them meet the requirements and standards they were supposed to attain in their subjects of study.

I discovered that creative writing (as well as the other arts) can be an invaluable tool and ally, helping students learn those "basic" skills and subjects with increased interest, enthusiasm, and success. For example, Siobhan's poem "Delicate Things Like" can be viewed as a vocabulary-development activity, finding examples and words to describe things that are *delicate*.

If creative writing can be seen and used as an integral part of teaching other areas of the curriculum, its value to the student can be greatly enhanced. Linden Jackson, a former student of mine, wrote, "Creative writing could be used to give some basic understanding to school subjects and arouse interests in each one, thus creating the desire to learn more about that subject."

purpose, purpose, purpose

Purpose can be defined as a meaningful and relevant reason for doing something that helps an individual reach a goal.

I hope you forgive me for harping on this point throughout the book, but I consider it that important: Never ever underestimate the importance and value of students' having a meaningful and relevant purpose for what they are studying. So much time, attention, effort, and energy is spent on skill development and so little on helping students find, understand, and agree upon a purpose for learning what they are studying. If more time were spent on helping students truly find and agree upon a purpose for learning some skill or subject matter, students—and teachers—would be much happier and more productive and successful.

Think about the areas in your life in which you have the most success; I'm sure that you are in agreement with a purpose related to those areas.

Creative writing can help create a purpose, to which a student agrees, for learning some subject matter or skill.

As you read the rest of this chapter, maintain as a basic viewpoint the concept that creative writing can be used to create a purpose that will help a student attain the knowledge, awareness, and applicable skill of any subject area.

the curriculum areas and creative writing

There are basically two ways to view the relationship and interaction between creative writing and subject areas of the curriculum. First, creative writing can help a student learn and improve in a subject area—writing leads to learning. Second, other subject areas can help involve and improve a student's creative writing—learning leads to writing. These two viewpoints are not mutually exclusive, and one often contributes to the other.

writing leads to learning

A student's interest in and involvement with creative writing can be used to introduce, review, practice, enhance, motivate, and help learn concepts, facts, and skills from various areas of the school curriculum.

Students are truly happiest when they have been productive and can share and demonstrate what they have produced (created). When a student has written about some part of a subject area, she has produced something that can be shared. Her pleasure of creation can and will be reflected in her having a positive attitude towards the subject matter, and the more positive one feels about something being studied, the more easily one can learn.

Students who use and create with the material they are studying are in a better position to learn because they are actively involved, not just passively receiving and accepting information. Active involvement will always be a superior learning approach to passive acceptance, because a student's interest and purpose for learning increases to the degree to which he is actively doing, using, and creating with the material being studied.

Linden Jackson wrote the following poem after discussion and study of drugs and drug abuse. It was his unique way of creating with the facts and viewpoints presented and discussed.

Ten Little Drug Addicts

Ten *little drug addicts*
feeling high
One took an overdose
then had to die
Nine *little drug addicts*
taking a smoke
One took a puff
and had a stroke
Eight *little drug addicts*
taking some hay
One took too much
then passed away
Seven *little drug addicts*
sniffing glue
One wanted more
then joined the dead too
Six *little drug addicts*
havin' a fix
One took more
and had death kicks
Five *more drug addicts*
Drinking alcoholic wine

One choked out
and fell off the line
Four *dizzy drug addicts*
on LSD
One died out
that left three
Three *rotten drug addicts*
with cocaine
One got killed
cause he jumped out a plane
Two *hairy drug addicts*
trying to push
One got busted
the other fell in a bush
One scared *drug addict*
thought he was in a shell
When he realized it
he was lying in hell
Now since you heard this
You might not want any too
BEWARE DRUG PUSHERS
DON'T GET YOU.

Creative writing can help a writer better understand and become more aware of the subject matter about which he is writing. To clearly communicate something requires a writer's personal awareness and understanding of that subject area, so the writer must study the material, organize it, and decide what and how to write about it.

The more times something is actively reviewed (and practiced), the more likely it will be learned and understood. The process of writing (researching, organizing, actively writing, editing, and rewriting) involves review of the subject matter being used in the creative writing project.

Finally, creative writing can broaden a student's knowledge, awareness and understanding of a subject area. As a writer gets involved in the creation of a written work, she may travel in directions she never imagined, new personal realizations and understandings about the subject may occur; new information may be found; new possibilities for using the material may come to light.

The following poem, written by Lynda Hardy, a junior-high-school student, reflects why and how creative writing can be used as an integral method in the learning of other curriculum areas:

The harvest moon which crept along the dark starlit heavens was
*   silhouetting against the crystal lake the figure of a*
crooked old woman.
The winter winds which swung through the dark thickening night
like a pendulum on a worn clock, howled in her ears for it
uncurled the haunting yelps of the vain dogs clamouring in
bewilderment.
As she clutched the old rifle that lay idly at her side, her
lonely voice echoed through the still forest winds:

No signs for whites only
*   ON THE FREEDOM TRAIN.*
No back doors for blacks
*   ON THE FREEDOM TRAIN.*
Train don't run off the track
*   ON THE FREEDOM TRAIN.*

THE LAW knew her as A FUGITIVE SLAVE.
HER PEOPLE knew her as MOSES.
HISTORY knows her as HARRIET TUBMAN.
*   JOURNEY*
*   TO*
*   THE*
*   PROMISED*
*   LAND.*

*   Lynda*

learning leads to writing

Students who have had positive experiences with creative writing look for, and welcome opportunities to write and subjects about which to write. As they study various curriculum areas, invariably something will appeal to them—that gleam in their creative spirit will appear, followed by an outflow of creative writing.

I have been amazed at what sparks some children and what their creative insights have produced. Science offers all kinds of possibilities for creative writing. The following is a wonderful example of science giving "birth" to a poem.

My Beginning

My body is throbbing
from head to toe,
Every square inch
feels the pain, you know.

My head feels swollen,
swollen as can be,
Everything around
looks blurry to me.

Now my body
is losing all of its feel,
I look around,
and nothing is real.

My mind grows dimmer,
but I catch a sight,
Like a beam in a tunnel
providing me light.

It comes to me whispering
of wisdom and good,
Just like any
special friend should.

It brings me an image
shining and clear,
As if trying to tell me
my beginning is near.

Brynn Bishop

As a teacher, your role is to open the door, or allow the door to remain open, to creative-writing activities based on what's being studied. Be accepting of and positive toward those written creations voluntarily done and shared by your students; encourage and motivate them to use creative writing to help express what they have learned.

Following up literature activities with creative writing is something I have often done; a literature unit on folk tales may be followed up with a writing activity based on the concepts discussed and learned. Whenever my class studied some aspect of literature—folk tale, tall tale, short story, poetry, fables, essays—invariably several students would show me their written creations *before* I initiated the idea of doing any writing. The following story, voluntarily written, was based on our discussion and reading of myths:

A Myth On How Deserts Were Formed

One day while the sun was blazing in the sky and the flowers and trees were standing awkwardly, a big heat wave came rumbling over the earth. All the things God made were sidling as if they were ill.

Then the sun became hotter and hotter, and insects, flowers and trees started to turn to dust. Millions and millions of insects and plants were turning in to dust.

After all the plants and insects were gone, God scanned the earth and found the insects and plants gone. Then he thought of something. He wanted to name it. He named it desert. *De* meaning dead, and *sert* meaning sorts.

The End

William

What kind of learning activity do you think inspired this poem by four year old Mathew Eaton?

> *I have a pocket*
> *In my pocket*
> *I go into space*
> *To be in a race*

What activity could have motivated Letty Heldt to write:

*A stream flows so gently
through a forest of green,
then into a pond of life.*

two principles for using creative writing as a learning tool

(All the principles and viewpoints of teaching creative writing discussed elsewhere in the book are still relevant.)

1. *Know the purpose for relating and using creative writing with other subject matter* before involving the student in the creative writing activity.

Creative writing can be used to help develop or maintain a positive attitude towards the subject area (which will motivate the student's involvement in studying the subject); to help a student gain familiarity with a subject; to review skills and knowledge (information and viewpoints) of a subject; to help a student learn new material on a subject.

2. *Direct students to a creative-writing activity that will accomplish the intended purpose.*

To gain familiarity with magnets and magnetism, the student can write a folk tale entitled, "Why Magnets Attract Things." (This writing activity could also help develop a positive attitude towards learning about magnetism.) Have the writer include what types of materials magnets attract.

To review skills and knowledge, the writer can write a science-fiction story, like, "Dr. Magno—the Magnetic Crusader," in which the writer will discuss the properties of magnets as a part of the story.

To help the writer better know and understand the subject matter, the writer could prepare a research paper on magnetism, written as a college student might do it—the organization and presentation of the material would be left up to the writer.

The key point is that you must know and understand your intended purpose in relating creative writing to some curriculum area and, through your designed activities, communicate this purpose to your students.

how to create or find ideas that will relate creative writing to other curriculum areas

For some, finding and creating writing ideas is a snap; if you are among this group, move on to the next section of the chapter. For others, it's like running through a quagmire of mud wearing lead-weighted boots; if your boots are muddy, read the following hints.

Always keep in mind *the purpose* of the creative writing activity, and find an idea appropriate to your purpose. For example, a creative-writing idea that helps review long vowel sounds is to have students write haiku poems in which the first words of each line have long vowel sounds.

Brainstorming for ideas by yourself, with students, or with any interested people may help. To brainstorm, you simply focus your attention and consideration on some particular area (for example, creative-writing activities to enhance the teaching of the geometric shapes like triangles, circles, and squares). All those involved in the brainstorming process come up with suggestions and ideas. There is no discussion of the idea. Invariably one idea sparks a flow of other ideas that feed off of, but change, the original idea. For example, the idea "If geometric shapes could talk" could easily lead to a composition idea: "A day in the life of a shape family." Keep adding to the list; when the list is complete, look over the ideas and select the ones that seem interesting and appropriate.

Find resources—books, filmstrips, magazines, people—that give ideas for writing activities, and adapt them as needed and appropriate (see list of resources at the end of the book). For example, in the book *Springboards to Creative Writing* (Fred Christensen, Creative Teaching Press, Inc., 1971), there is the idea of "What's in the Box?" to help stimulate a writer's imagination and use the student's senses. This idea could be adapted to help a student learn about new geometric shapes by asking the student, "What would happen if a square gave birth to an octagon?" (The student will have to look up and understand what an octagon is to participate in this activity.)

Look through a subject text or other related material for the curriculum area, with the stress on how you can adapt elements to a creative-writing activity. For example, while looking at the geometry section of a math book, the pictures of various geometric shapes may spark some ideas, like "Write a story to explain why the triangle has three points."

Adapt ideas that you've seen or used in the past to a particular need in the present. These ideas can be found in any of your previous experiences, not just those related to the subject or to creative writing. For example, having seen various-shaped jewelry might spark the creative-writing idea for an essay on "Which geometric shape is the most aesthetically pleasing?" or "If shapes could talk, they would tell you the prettiest shape is _____."

Observe art, literature, music, your environment with the intention of picking up creative-writing ideas as related to a specific curriculum area. For example, looking at a copy of Roget's Thesaurus might stimulate an idea to write about the geometric shapes with their definitions all mixed up, so that a circle is defined as a three-sided figure formed by connecting three points not in a straight line and a triangle is defined as a plane curve everywhere equidistant from a fixed point, the center. Students can write a story about triangular tires and circular pyramids. These hints for finding and creating writing ideas are appropriate for students as well as teachers. It's really nice having students whose imagination, sense of adventure, and humor have not been quashed. They could be the source of your ideas. Every year I had at least one student, and usually more, who was a veritable fountain of weird, zany, appropriate, innovative, and imaginative ideas that would help spark others into writing.

creative writing and research

A few words on research are a must, as the creative-writing process inherently involves research (from the superficial to the profound).

I have a friend, a professional novelist, who in preparation for his novels spends months researching and studying material he intends to include in his books. He will travel to foreign countries he plans to use in his story and will do extensive research through books, interviews, and other sources.

When I speak of research, I refer to the investigation of and inquiry about a topic of interest and concern. Creative writing gives a writer a strong purpose for actively investigating and inquiring about some subject area (not with just an "I'd-better-do-it-to-get-a-good-grade" attitude, which results in little actual interest or involvement by the writer-researcher).

What the specific creative-writing project is about will help determine the type and extent of the research to be done. It might involve research by the writer into her personal feelings and understandings; it might involve the writer's observation of her environment and others in the environment; it could include extensive library research. For example, a theme like "The Perfect World" could lead to research on such subjects as government, economics, religion, education, and architecture.

The following poem is the result of Siobhan's personal research into herself and her environment. It expresses her truths, feelings, and beliefs which resulted from that research.

This Is The Ghetto

My mind is far away—
But I'm careful of the way I sway,
As I pass the building where everyone stays
This is the Ghetto—These are the Slums.
And there's the garbage,
stagnant water—glass and mess
a dead dog across the street—
I just saw a rat—
This is the Ghetto—These are the Slums.
Kids in the halls
On the steps
Out in the street—
On the block—on the corner,
Some are dirty—snotty nosed
nappy hair—smelly clothes
Others—clean, bebopping bad
"What's happen' Dad?"
This is the Ghetto—These are the Slums.
Cops are common—when they ain't wanted—

Whites are scarce, though known—
And the junkies—Oh, the junkies
Old and young—copping down, down, down
shooting till doomsday—people are scared
What can be done? You tell me.
Swarming like ants—like roaches in the bathroom—2 o'clock in the
morning when you gotta go—you turn on the light and they're—One's
crawling over your big toe
This is the Ghetto—These are the Slums.
I remember when the old ladies and tall half-bald men used to come
They would walk down the street—looking at the houses, but not on my
side
They held leaflets and wore spectacles
White people—I wonder what they thought they were really doing.
We would show off and make a lot of noise—
And as we got older we would shout after them—
"This is the Ghetto—These are the Slums!"
"Do you like what you see?"
I don't.
But now they don't come anymore.
They aren't welcome by most—I guess they know that.
They seem out of place—they are.
And the people—how about them?
They just live here.
Their kids go to the school down the street—sometimes.
They look at the dirt and keep walking
They smell the rank odors and keep walking
They know who the pusher is and keep walking
They know who shot him and keep walking
They know who raped her and keep walking
They know who mugged the crippled white man and keep walking
And the roaches climb,
And the junkie snorts.
And the whores tease,
And the rats run.
And the kids fight,
And the walls peel.
And the hall stinks,
And the Check comes.

And the muggers run,
And the Cops shoot.
This *is the Ghetto*—These *are the Slums.*

Siobhan

Expansive tomes have been written on proper research techniques and tools (see bibliography). I will cover some of the basic things the creative writer should know about researching.

The creative writer should know as specifically as possible the kinds of information needed (the who, what, where, why, when, and how). He should be aware of the best sources and ways of getting the information (from direct personal experience observation of others or information from others—these are more extensively covered in the chapter on essays). He should learn how to select out key facts, ideas, examples, and quotes that are relevant to the creative-writing project.

And he should know how to organize the research material for the creative-writing project. The ability to outline is important in this step. The key to outlining is knowing the main idea, identifying and differentiating between the major and minor support ideas, and selecting the details, illustrations, and examples to be used.

Creative-writing projects helped motivate some of the most successful research projects in which I was able to involve my students, when they learn how to do research, as well as learn the subject matter they were researching. One year my fourth-grade class was assigned to do a presentation for the rest of the school for Dental Health Week. The challenge that confronted us was how to write a play that would be of interest, entertain, and convey the necessary information about Dental Health Week. The class was about as enthusiastic as the time the librarian had them write one hundred times, "I shall not talk in the library."

Any request to do the needed research for writing the play would have been doomed to groans, grunts, and grimaces, not the ideal attitude with which to begin a creative-writing or research activity.

The class reluctantly began to brainstorm for ideas about the play. Someone called out "Superheroes"; one boy, Victor, took the idea a step further and called out, "Decay Man versus Supertooth." That was the magical idea; the class got excited about doing a play based on the concept of "Decay Man versus Supertooth."

It was easy to get them to do the necessary research. We discussed sources of information, what types of information we should look for, reviewed note-taking and how to find and select information and ideas that related to our topic.

When the research was done, we discussed the key concepts we wanted to communicate through our play; they included how to avoid abusing teeth, proper care of teeth, and some basic information about teeth. We then decided how we would present and support these concepts in our play.

The play was a great, great success. We communicated our message in a way that the audience both enjoyed and understood. It was so successful that the principal, whose office was near the school auditorium, had to stop a meeting because the laughter and involvement of the audience was so distracting. At the conclusion of the play he presented each child in the class with a toothbrush (he had rushed one of the secretaries out to buy them during the play) and joined in the rousing ovation given the class.

That was a most successful research project.

creative writing
and the language arts

The language arts—speaking, listening, reading, and writing—are an obvious curriculum area in which creative writing can be used as a learning tool. A good creative-writing program can only help develop a greater understanding of, awareness of, skill in, and interest in all the language arts. When the student writes he is actively taking responsibility for creating with and using words and the skills and knowledge that are part of the language arts curriculum.

Creative-writing projects that integrate into other language-arts areas can focus the student's attention on reviewing work previously done; using material currently being studied; preparing and motivating for work yet to come.

The creative-writing activities could be based on an evaluation of the needs and abilities of students in the language arts. For example, if a student still needs help in understanding the rules of punctuation after completing a unit of study on punctuation, a creative-writing activity like "When the comma wanted to be a period" would be a productive way of practicing and reviewing the skills learned. To introduce certain listening skills, an appropriate creative-writing project would be an essay on "Where the sounds go" (after having listened to specific sounds presented by the teacher).

creative writing and reading

"Dear Reader,

We have enjoyed making this book. We hope you enjoy reading it.

Love,

Billy, Theyna, Paul, Sean, Mark, Robert, Fred, Herbert, Tara, Arnel, Desiree, Anthony, James N., James S., Rosemary, Alvin, and Mrs. Solari"

This is the opening of a book, *Our Class Book (The Greatest Stories in the World),* created by third-grade students in a remedial-reading class. Cam Solari, the teacher, recognized how valuable an asset creative writing could be in teaching reading and made it a major part of her very successful reading program.

Creative writing has also been an important part of my reading program. I had one fifth grade student, Eric, who was turned off to reading because of his difficulty in learning how to read. One day as I heard him talking to a friend, I wrote down some of the things he was saying; he had a very expressive speaking style. I put his words on several sheets of paper (each sheet had one sentence) and made a book out of his words. The next day I called him up to my desk and showed him the book. "How would you like to read the book with me?" I asked.

He glanced at it and said with the enthusiasm of a man about to be lynched, "Sure."

I began to read the book to him: "You should have seen me sky for that ball."

A look of curiosity appeared on Eric's face.

"Me, Clarence, and Frank beat those suckers so bad, they had their tongues touching the ground."

Eric's mouth seemed to drop to the floor.

I read that page again. Eric stared at the words, and blurted out, "Hey, I said that."

"You're right, those are your words. I copied what you were telling Danny yesterday about your basketball game."

Eric had no problem understanding what the book was about; he wanted me to read the book to him (which I did), then took the book back to his seat. I kept glancing at him for the next half-hour; his eyes never left his book except to ask someone to help him with a word.

From that day on, Eric wrote many books, often dictating the words to me or another student, but many times (especially later in the school year) writing the books himself (with whatever help he needed and requested).

I had another student, Donald, who was a skilled reader, but who rarely opened a book unless there was an assignment to be done. He wrote a short story for a creative-writing project that was really outstanding. I made a point of giving him both private and public recognition for his writing, and others who read or heard his story were equally as validating. That validation sparked a creative flow and spirit in Donald, and he began writing short stories on his own.

To take advantage of the situation, I found a book of Black folk tales and showed it to Donald. I suggested he might get some good ideas for future stories from the book. He read the book in one night, and the next day asked me if I knew of any others he might read. I smiled and said, "No, there are no more books you can read," as I handed him another book I had found at home.

I cite these examples to illustrate how valuable creative writing can be to a reading program. The affinity a student will feel for words and reading will increase as she has success in writing (using and creating with words). When someone has interest and success in creating in some activity, there is a natural inclination to feel closer, more at ease, and more willing to confront that whole area of activity. In addition, at the risk of belaboring the point, a student learns best when she is actively involved and creating in a learning experience of which she agrees to be part. Writing is a creative end of reading.

Think about something you recently became interested in and successful at doing. Do you find yourself more receptive to and interested in reading about the subject, finding out about the success of others, and getting viewpoints and information about that area?

I started running about three years ago and began to devour books on the subject. I watched others run with a more discerning and interested eye, comparing what they did with my style and technique of running.

Success and interest in creative writing will invariably lead to a student's increased awareness, understanding, and interest in reading (both his own writing and the writing of others). As the teacher, you must decide how to best use the student's interest and ability in writing to improve his reading ability.

Creative writing and reading go hand in hand—reading is enhanced by writing, and writing is enhanced by reading. Each can help develop skills, understandings, and awarenesses of how words can be used and how to use words, as well as motivate a student's interest and involvement in the other.

I've never known a writer who couldn't read, and a reader who couldn't write.

suggested creative writing ideas for specific curriculum areas

I present the following ideas as a springboard for you. Observe the needs, interests, and abilities of your students and adapt or use the ideas as you feel best. I emphasize again, know exactly what your purpose is when helping a child relate creative writing to a curriculum area.

language arts

Any writing activity will, in some way, relate to the language arts. All the writing ideas presented throughout the book are relevant activities. You can decide how to adapt the ideas for a particular purpose that relates to the language-arts curriculum and the needs of the student.

For example, the expository essay can be used in a variety of ways.

To help the student differentiate fact from opinion through *listening,* have her become an undercover reporter. Have her distinguish between fact and opinions by listening to various conversations at lunch, then write a gossip column based on what she overheard. She should only include opinions she heard expressed and not any facts.

To help develop the *reading* skill of finding and using the appropriate references when seeking information about a subject, have the student prepare a magazine article for possible publication in an established magazine. Base the article on a topic of interest the student would like to research.

To help the student learn how to effectively deliver a verbal communication *(speaking)*, he can write an essay on all the wrong ways of speaking with another. This can be done in a humorous vein and will help the student develop an awareness of what to do by writing what not to do.

To help develop *writing* skills, any of the three preceding ideas would be appropriate, depending on the purpose of the writing activity. You could focus the writer's attention on concise word use and limit her essay exactly to 109 words.

Here's an example of a poem that reviews antonyms.

Life

Life
What is it?

. . .
Thu! Stop! Think! Think!

. . .
Stop thinking of what they think.
What do you think?

I think it's priceless.

It is alone.
It is hard,
It is easy.
It is happiness,
It is sad.
It is powerful,
It is weak.
It is good,
It is bad.
It is love,
It is not wanted.

It is rich,
It is poor.
It is crazy,
It is quiet.
It is wicked,
It is virtuous.

Life can be anything to anybody.
   . . .

                                        Thu Nguyen

There should prove no problem in deciding how to integrate creative writing with the area of language arts.

math

Write a folk tale telling how numbers (or any mathematical concept) came to be.

Create a math dictionary, with the definitions in the writer's own words.

Write a poem (decide on what form would be appropriate) about the concept being studied: a love poem to an equilateral triangle, a limerick about division. Here's a rhyming poem about distance facts:

I can now be happy and crack a smile,
I know 5,280 feet equals one mile
I just learned something really neat,
One yard has three feet.

Make up jokes and riddles using math facts—Why did they call the lame dog "Yard"? He could only use three feet.

Create an advertising campaign that will help a student understand why it's important to learn some math facts and concepts.

Write a story on what it's like to be a _____ (fill in whatever mathematical term is appropriate).

Write a letter to the math book's publisher explaining what is liked and not liked about the math book, with specific reference to mathematical concepts and how they are presented.

Create various kinds of word problems that involve the math concepts and facts being learned.

Create a "wanted" poster for missing geometric shapes, describing what they look like, with appropriate illustrations and examples of what they have done and can do.

Write a play about how division helps multiplication find the missing answer.

social studies

Write a news broadcast for a particular period of time—Sunday, December 7, 1941, tape-record it, and present it to the class.

Change the outcome or facts of some famous event and write an essay—If *Abraham Lincoln had a Bulletproof Shield at Ford's Theater;* If *England Won The Revolutionary War.*

Write captions for photos of various events, places, or world figures.

Make up a quiz in which the answers are given and the reader has to supply the questions. Base the answers on what is currently being studied, or have one student make it up in preparation for the class study (so the class will have to supply the correct questions as they study the particular topic).

Write letters to a newspaper editor about some current world, national, or local event or situation.

Do a radio advertisement, to be taped, on why visitors should come to some part of the world being studied.

Write a presentation for a television show based on a person or group of people being studied (actually mail it to one of the networks).

Develop a scrapbook, with appropriate descriptions and explanations about some person, place, or event.

Write a diary as if you were some famous historical character.

Write an editorial about some aspect of what is currently being studied.

science

Write myths to explain why there is snow (or any other scientific phenomena).

Write a handbook explaining how to administer first aid.

Prepare a consumer report on the most nutritious foods to buy and what foods to avoid.

Pretend you have interviewed some famous scientist; list the questions asked and how he or she responded.

Create a science-fiction story based on the scientific truths being studied.

Write a sonnet from an amoeba to a paramecium.

Write a thank-you note to the rain for all it does that is helpful; write a no-trespassing sign to the rain, for all it does that is destructive.

Write a list of scientific predictions that is to be sealed for twenty years, when it will be opened by the writer to see how accurate the predictions were.

If a magnet could talk, what would it say?

Write roses-are-red poems:

> *Roses are red,*
> *Bees live in a hive,*
> *The heart pumps blood*
> *And helps keep us alive.*
>
> *Roses are red,*
> *A lawn has grass*
> *Water is liquid*
> *But air is gas.*

How well you are able to relate and apply creative writing to other content areas of the curriculum can be an opportunity to test and validate your creative ability. I wish you good times in the reading, enjoyment, and fulfillment that comes when your creative ingenuity has helped a student become more involved, aware, and understanding of a curriculum area because of her creative writing.

nine

when students don't want to participate in creative writing

When

When thoughts are black, and voices cry purple,
Laughter is bitter, and tears run free,
When eyes stare cold, and hearts are shattered,
And people are empty,
When tree leaves are grey, blue seas are slime,
And birds are frozen,
When the air is dense, the wind is still,
And the earth grows thin and jagged,
When skies fall heavy, and stars are tin,
And the sun goes away,

Life is done.

Siobhan

I hope the images created by Siobhan's poem will not be symbolic of your students' feelings and attitudes toward creative writing. Yet, thoughts *are* black and voices *do* cry purple when creative writing has not been properly taught or presented to students.

The information and viewpoints that follow are presented to help you help those students who reflect a "life-is-done" attitude when the teacher attempts to involve them in creative writing.

what is the problem? what to do

There are two basic principles to know, understand, and apply in all situations in which a student does not want to participate in creative writing:

1. *Communicate with the student to find out why she doesn't want to write.*

William James wrote, "The most immutable barrier in nature is between one man's thoughts and another's."

When a student decides she doesn't wish to write (either generally, or for a specific topic, purpose, activity, or time period), she is the only person who really knows why. The answer rests in her thoughts. The teacher's role is to create a bridge that will overcome the barrier between thoughts, to find out whether there is any problem or difficulty causing her reluctance to write.

When I conduct workshops for educators in the creative arts, I always involve them in a creative activity; often it's a writing activity based on the "peace is" lesson discussed in Chapter 5. The participants are asked to voluntarily read and share their written creations with the group.

I remember one particular workshop in which a woman seemed to be lifting an eighty-pound weight as she raised her hand, volunteering to read her creation. She read her thoughts on peace; they were beautifully written. She then commented, "This is the first time I've wanted to write in years and share my thoughts with another person, let alone a whole group. I really want to thank you (referring to me) for making the space safe enough for me to really communicate to other people."

She was glowing.

I spoke with her afterwards and asked what she meant when she said I "made the space safe for her to communicate." She replied, "I knew that whatever I said would be listened to and received with sincere interest and that no matter what I said you would have accepted and understood. I was *not* worried about being belittled or told I was wrong. I really knew you could see things from my point of view." She ended with a warm hug and pleasant kiss on my cheek (a nice fringe benefit from creating a safe space).

Her statement sums up what I believe has to occur to overcome the barrier between the thoughts of two people, especially student and teacher.

2. *Do not coerce a student to do creative writing.*

In gathering material for this book, I prepared a survey. One question was, "What should a teacher *not* do when teaching, motivating, or involving someone in creative writing?"

A typical response was, "I think a teacher should *not* push a child who does not enjoy creative writing."

Not to push a student really means to allow him the freedom to say "no." Any creative art form has as its basic thrust the decision by the artist to create (which implies the right of the artist to decide not to create).

How do *you* feel when you are forced or coerced into doing something, especially in an area where the choice of participation should be entirely yours?

some situations
and how to handle them

What follows is a listing of some of the possible reasons a student wouldn't want to write, with some possible ways to overcome them.

It's up to you to communicate with your students to find out the true reason, and it's up to you to decide what should be done to best handle a particular situation.

the student has no purpose for writing   Help the writer find a purpose with which she agrees that will spark her creative energy. See Chapter 3 for a more complete discussion related to purpose.

the student has no interest for a specific creative-writing topic, project, or activity or no interest in general for creative writing   If a student has no interest in a topic, project, or activity, she should not have to write about it; help her find another topic in which she has genuine interest. If she has no interest in doing any creative writing, help her find another art form that is of more interest to her.

One caution—be certain her explanation, "I'm just not interested," is not a cover-up for some other underlying, more basic reason, such as she really lacks belief in her ability to actually write creatively. Some of these more basic reasons are mentioned below.

her creative-writing ability has been invalidated at some point in the past Invalidation can have a devastating impact on a student's ability and willingness to create. That invalidation can be very subtle— "Well, I guess you tried your best"—or blatant—"That stinks." Can you remember a time when you created or did something of which you were proud, and a person belittled your accomplishment in some way, or expressed a negative reaction to it? How did you feel?

There are many ways someone can respond to invalidation: laugh at the person's ignorance, attempt to kick him in the head (I know one fourth-grader who created a papier-mache puppet of which she was proud; when her teacher scolded her for not following directions and said the puppet was no good, the student got so angry she started hitting the teacher with the puppet), become apathetic about ever creating again. Far, far too often invalidation from another has led to a decision to stop creating in an art form or activity.

Try to find out when he was last doing well and wanted to write creatively. Ask whether anyone at that time had indicated in some way that what he wrote was no good, told him he was doing something wrong, or in any way made less of his creative talent. If someone or some incident comes to his mind, let him know that that person or thing was a @#$%%¢$##$ (not necessarily in that language). Often just finding out what happened to stop his creative spirit will help revitalize him.

Make a point of validating what he does right, and comment on his strengths as a writer. Help him regain belief in his ability to create, because that ability has never left but has only been covered by the residue of invalidation—anger, fear, resentment, apathy, and self-invalidation (if someone goes into agreement with another's invalidation, it becomes self-invalidation).

the student feels inadequate because of poor technical reading and/or writing skills (grammar, spelling, punctuation) Give whatever help she needs and asks for while writing: allow her to dictate a story; help her spell words for which she asks help; let her work with another, more technically advanced student. Help her work on the basic skills independent of creative-writing activities.

the student does not understand or is confused about something related to creative writing (in general or in relation to some specific activity or project) Too often teachers assume that a student knows and understands more than he does (especially the words and vocabulary used to discuss or explain things). I cannot stress strongly enough the importance of not allowing confusions to develop that are caused by lack of understanding in how to execute a particular step of some activity. The whole area of study is involved. (Some of the best and most usable research and technology in the area of study has been developed by L. Ron Hubbard, an educator and philosopher. I urge you to read *The Basic Study Manual*[1] for more information.)

Find out what the student's problem is. Perhaps there are some words she does not understand—the student can't write a seventeen-syllable haiku poem because she does not know what a syllable is; if she is having trouble writing a quatrain, she may not have fully understood what couplets are.

I will stress again that not fully understanding words or steps in learning is a major contributor to a student's having problems and difficulties with creative writing (or any art form).

his inadequate vocabulary development prevents him from finding the words he needs and wants to express his thoughts Help him develop his vocabulary through word files, word games, discussions about words, or whatever activity you can find or create that will help him build his vocabulary. You can help him use a thesaurus or the dictionary to find words to express his thoughts.

---

[1]*The Basic Study Manual* is available from any Applied Scholastics Incorporated organizations found throughout the world. For more information write, Applied Scholastics, Inc., 955 S. Western Ave., Los Angeles, CA 90006.

the student lacks ideas about which to write   Provide the student with increased opportunities for building her experience base, from which she can draw ideas. Trips, more reading (to her and by her), discussions, watching and discussing movies and television can serve this purpose.

Help her develop her ability to observe—to use her senses—and perceive things from her observation: have her observe a particular classmate and list the things he does and his apparent reasons for doing those things; have her close her eyes and describe the sounds heard as they occur.

he lacks ideas for a specific creative-writing topic, activity, or project   Brainstorm with the student for ideas related to the activity. Turn him on to possible sources of ideas: people who know about the topic, books, magazines, other students' writing. Have him observe something related to the project, focusing attention on what would be a good idea to write about or use.

you—there may be some things you are doing that turn the student off to creative writing   Evaluate yourself. Question students about their feelings and thoughts concerning your teaching of creative writing; establish criteria to evaluate yourself and be as objective as possible in that evaluation.

Here are some criteria for evaluation you might use:

1. Do you create a safe space in which the students can communicate (that is, validate their creative efforts and avoid invalidation or showing disapproval of their effort)?

2. Do you assume the student knows and understands more than she really does (especially the vocabulary you use to discuss and explain things)?

3. Do you have and express genuine interest in your students' creative efforts?

4. Do you provide opportunities for the writer to share his work with others?

5. Do you approach creative writing with enthusiasm and the belief that every student can write creatively? Do you express these feelings to your students?

6. Do you help provide the experiences from which students can draw ideas for writing creatively (this includes vocabulary building, oral expression, trips, discussions, reading to the student and by the student)?

7. Do you teach the basic writing skills separate from creative writing?

8. Do you allow students the freedom *not* to write?

9. Do you actively help a student as he expresses the need and willingness to be helped?

10. Do you help a student find a genuine purpose for creative writing with which she is in agreement?

11. Do you help motivate a student's writing by helping him find topics that interest and concern him?

12. Do you allow a student the freedom to decide how and what to do with her written creation?

13. Do you provide adequate time and opportunity for students to write?

I'll let the final words for this section be those of Ann Arthur, a former student of mine, who wrote: "I write for the pure pleasure of it. For me, writing is a relaxer, a thought organizer. What I can't or won't say aloud, I can write down. *After all, paper doesn't rush or interrupt, and better still, it can't yell back at you!"*

ten

four sample lessons and activities for creative writing

The following sample lessons and activities are intended to help you generate ideas and plans to develop creative writing lessons and activities. What you plan should be based on the needs, interests, and abilities of your class and students, as well as *your* particular interests, strengths, and purposes.

advice for planning and creating lessons and activities

The most important piece of advice I can give about planning is that you must clearly understand what you intend the outcome of any lesson or activity to be. There could be many results:

Students knowing how to create a specific form of writing, like haiku poetry.

Students being able to use a new tool for creative writing, like using metaphors.

Students being better able to use certain skills related to creative writing, like brainstorming and observation.

Students having increased understanding of various curriculum areas which have been combined with a creative-writing activity, such as creating a forty-seven-word story based on the week's spelling words.

Students having a more positive attitude for creative writing, being willing to share and validate the work of particular students.

A written creation being produced about which the student can feel good about, such as writing on a theme of interest to the student.

Other things I have found helpful in creating lessons and activities are: not assuming students know and understand more than they do; trying to make the content relevant and meaningful to the students; showing them what they will have as a result of completing a particular activity (in doing a lesson on "wanted" posters, I would at the start of the lesson show the students posters already done by other students; I found doing this is a wonderful motivator and helps increase the understanding of what's to be done) actively working to get the students' agreement for doing the writing activity; being enthusiastic and interested in what the lesson or activity is about; indicating to the students how they can benefit from the activity, thus helping to create a purpose with which the students agree.

an activity for physically, emotionally, or mentally handicapped students

I want to make three points about involving handicapped students in creative writing:

1. All the gains, values, and principles that apply to "normal" students also apply to the handicapped.

2. Gear the writing activity and its purpose to the specific needs, interests, and actual (not apparent) limitations of the student. A blind student cannot describe a scene in visual terms, but he can utilize the heightened sensitivity of his other senses to describe the sounds, smells, and feelings of a scene. A student physically unable to write can dictate his story. Deaf students might first deal with concrete ideas rather than abstract ones, until their vocabularies have grown to the point at which they can associate abstract concepts with the words they know.

3. When involving handicapped students in creative writing, it's very important that their lack of technical skills in writing does not stop their creative effort, flow and thought. Let them dictate, or write sloppily, or misspell, but validate their creative effort, flow, and thought. Provide whatever extra help the students specifically need to accommodate their handicaps—have a blind student smell a flower and tell him several words that describe the aroma, then allow him to select the words he would like to use in describing the flower's scent. There might have to be more teacher direction and involvement in the creative process for handicapped students than "normal" students.

The following project was an expanded creative experience which involved creative writing, done with elementary-school students who were physically and emotionally handicapped.

A filmmaker, Ralph Olson, worked with a special class, and with the help of their teacher, helped the children develop a creative story that they filmed.

The teacher felt having her students work in a group situation was helpful because the stronger students could provide a model and stimulus for those who had difficulty in doing creative work; because everyone identified with the group, they all could feel they had a part in the creation of the material.

1. The children were helped in selecting an idea. In this particular situation, because of the variety of handicapped children in the class, it was felt that the teacher should select the idea based on what she felt was important in the lives of the children.

Since the children spend much of their free time racing each other in wheelchairs and walkers, it was natural to evolve a story around the theme, "The Great Race."

2. The teacher proceeded, with the filmmaker, to direct the children's thinking by asking them a series of questions:

"Would you like to create a story about a race?" (The answer was an overwhelming "yes".)
"Do you want good guys and bad guys?"

"What kinds of good guys do you want? Ones who always win? Giving and kind? Helpful?"

"What kinds of bad guys? A cheater? A name-caller? Mean?"

The teacher continued to guide the creative process, giving the possible choices from which the students would select. The ideas for the film evolved with the choices made by the students.

"What do you want the characters to do? Should the cheater lose or win?"

During the year the teacher had stressed that trying was more important than actually winning, so it was natural for the class to include in the story a third character who would represent the disadvantaged person who tried hard but lost. They eventually came up with this plan:

Good guy wins.

Cheater loses.

Someone tries hard but loses.

To further develop the story, the teacher asked the students to imagine themselves as the winner and decide what they would do with the prize money (keep it, give it away, give part of it away, something else). The teacher did not impose moral judgments on the children but instead made them feel safe enough to say what they *really* would do.

The teacher took the class's ideas and put them in the sequence of a story, drew a story board, and then read the story to the class so changes could be made and other ideas added.

The next step was to bring the story alive. The students researched race cars in books and then each designed an individual car. The teacher took their designs and cut them, on a larger scale, out of heavy, two-sided cardboard. The children supervised the adults who brought their designs to life, making suggestions as needed. The students decorated and painted the cardboard cars themselves.

Actors were selected on the basis of interest and who the teacher believed could handle each role. The dialogue of the film was kept simple; ideas were generated by the class and written by the teacher.

This extensive creative project resulted in a multitude of learning experiences that resulted in the delight and excitement of the students as they saw themselves, and what they had created, in the completed film.

haiku: being a writer, the environment, choral speaking

This lesson involves teaching a new poetic form, haiku poetry; utilizing the student's environment; helping develop a positive attitude towards creative writing; presenting the viewpoint of *being a writer* when writing, not just a student who is writing; doing choral speaking based on the poetry written; possibly interrelating poetry with other curriculum areas.

lesson steps
(this lesson took forty-five minutes
with a sixth-grade class)

1. Briefly review and discuss the purpose of creative writing (to communicate thoughts, feelings, and beliefs to create a certain effect on the reader, or whatever you and the class feel the purpose is).

2. Discuss the different kinds of writing—essays, poetry, stories.

3. Introduce haiku. Read a couple of examples of haiku poetry and discuss what it is—a Japanese seventeen-syllable poem that deals with a writer's response to something in nature.

4. Review what a syllable is (a whole "pronunciation part" of a word, in some cases an entire word) and how to figure out the number of syllables in a word—place a hand on your chin and say a word, and each time your chin goes down you've said a syllable. Practice this for a few words.

5. Show the line pattern of a haiku poem:

First line	— five syllables
Second line	— seven syllables
Third line	— five syllables

Write a group poem, reviewing the line pattern. Ask the class to check for the correct number of syllables when someone gives a line for the poem.

The major concern of this lesson is that students understand what a haiku poem is and how to write one. The aesthetic flow and presentation can be worked on in future activities.

6. Have the class copy the haiku pattern and the class poem. This can be used as a reference by the students.

7. Discuss how a poet may write and create his poetry—finding something to write about as a result of what he observes and perceives, selecting the poetic form in which to write, and finally writing his poem.

8. Stress the concept of *being a poet* when writing poetry, not a sixth-grade student, a boy or a girl, eleven years old. Have them practice being a poet by walking, sitting, and observing as they feel a poet would.

9. Take the class into the yard. Remind them about being a poet and stress that no one is to intrude on the personal space of anyone else for ten minutes—no speaking, touching, or communicating in any way.

10. Discuss observing things in the environment with the intention of finding something that goes "click" and inspires the writing of a haiku poem.

11. Have the students walk around on their own, observing the environment. Observe the students, helping as needed. At some point find a place to sit and write your own poem. Be ready for the poets who will come up to you to share their poetry and want to read yours. Acknowledge their creations, and find something to validate in each poem. If a poet has not followed the correct pattern, ask her to check her poem for any break in the syllable pattern; stress that she try to keep the same thought and feeling she originally intended as she corrects the poem for technical mistakes.

12. Have the class return to the room. Collect the poems of the writers who would like to share their creations with the group. Read a few to the class, but do not tell who wrote the poem being read. Have the class guess who the poet is. After three guesses ask the poet to stand (she has the right not to stand and not be identified).

13. Select, or have the class select, three poems to be read as a part of a choral speaking activity. Review the basics of choral speaking—starting, continuing and finishing together; staying at the same level of volume as everyone else; following the leader.

The writer of each poem, or someone they select, should lead the group. Record their choral speaking, and play it back to the class—they will love it!

from brainstorming to poetry

This lesson helps students learn how to receive information, combine it with their own experience and point of view, and then produce an original idea or new combinations of images.

The lesson develops vocabulary; helps combine writing with the arts of dance, photography, and music; motivates the writing of poetry—free verse and cinquains; provides opportunity for evaluation of written work; utilizes group interaction; provides opportunities for sharing what has been created; involves using the technique of brainstorming.

lesson steps

1. Select photos that show scenes from nature.

2. Have the students, in small groups, look at a few photos.

3. Have the students in each group list words and thoughts stimulated by the photos. All answers are to be acknowledged without any evaluation or ridicule.

The groups are to look at the photos in terms of actions, colors, shapes, descriptive words, spaces (directions, sizes, levels), time elements (slow, fast, regular, irregular), nouns, feelings and relationships.

4. After the group involvement, each student is given an individual photo and asked to go to a spot in the room or environment in which he or she can be alone.

5. They are to write down as many words as they can in a given time period (five to ten minutes). The time limit helps to push them into responding quickly, without giving them time to create artificial barriers like:

"I can't spell";
"I can't think of anything to put down";
"I don't like this picture";
"This is too hard."

6. The students then exchange photos and idea sheets (this is to have the thinking of another person enhance their own ideas and expand their images).

7. The students get their original photos and idea sheets back, look through the lists, and begin building combinations of words, eliminating some and developing others.

8. In this particular lesson the students are asked to take their ideas and write a cinquain poem (a form of poetry they already know). The following is a brainstorm list from a photo of clouds and sky at the break of a storm:

mysterious	fluffy	soft as a feather
colorful	powerful	gloomy
ocean storm	heaven	King of Gods
beautiful	God's place	evening sky
noisy	Golden Gate	
darkness		

Here are two poems based on the same photo:

Power
Mysterious
Moving very slowly
Big, enormous, humongous
Real strong

Ken Seaman

The weather is full of nice sounds.
It rumbles
It splishes
It tumbles
it splashes
and it crashes

Robin Watson

9. To extend the creative experience, the students divide into groups of threes and fours, reading their poetry to one another.

10. The group decides on one poem to be used to shape a dance that develops the ideas of the poem.

The dance is to have a strong beginning, middle, and end in a group shape.

After some rehearsal, these dances are informally performed for the class, with the class giving suggestions to the performing group. The group then reworks the dance, and in some cases the poems may be given a variation to better stimulate the movement.

11. The final presentation involves the reading of the poems, the sharing of the photos, and the dances performed with simple musical accompaniment that captures the flavor and rhythm of the pieces.

take advantage of a situation

Throughout the year things will occur that could motivate creative writing. The following lesson steps are meant to serve as a guide to help you take advantage of appropriate situations to develop writing activities with your students.

lesson steps

1. Be on the alert for the moment when something occurs that captures the interest, concern, or enthusiasm of your students: a current event; a school or classroom situation; something that involves individual students. You will know when that moment has arrived. The death of Dr. Martin Luther King Jr.; a student's brother dying from a drug overdose; winning the school fund-raising contest; the day our snake disappeared—these are but a few of the things that generated creative-writing activities for students in my classes.

2. Discuss with your students whatever it is that sparked their interest, concern, or enthusiasm. This discussion helps formulate ideas, questions, feelings, and information and helps the student focus on something in the topic that they find particularly relevant and meaningful.

3. If possible and practical in terms of the time and effort required to find appropriate material, read something to the class related to the topic of concern and interest. For the death of Dr. Martin Luther King Jr., I read the closing section of his "I Had a Dream" speech; when the snake disappeared I read a poem titled, "The Bug-a-Boo Snake."

4. What you are looking for at this point is a bright idea that would be relevant, meaningful, and help motivate your students to write. If nothing clicks for you, ask a couple of your more creative students, or even the entire class, what can be done. For Dr. King's death, students wrote personal poetry and essays that were sent to his family; when the snake disappeared, quatrains were written that were sent as warnings to classes throughout the school. For example:

> *Jerri is missing and moves kind of slow,*
> *If you see him please let us know.*
> *Be kind to him, for goodness sake,*
> *He can't help being a two-foot snake.*

5. Do whatever is appropriate to follow up and successfully accomplish that bright idea. This might be a good time to introduce some new material or review and practice things already learned.

eleven

all kinds of ideas

This section of the book has two purposes: to provide ideas you can use in your creative writing program; and more importantly, to help you generate your own ideas.

As you read the ideas, think about how they could be used or changed for your particular creative-writing program. Brainstorm and create your own ideas for the thirteen areas I shall cover.

I have not attempted to make these idea lists exhaustive—I've cited several books in the resource section that include an abundance of creative writing ideas—rather, I have attempted to include a variety of ideas that will stimulate your thinking and creation of ideas you can use.

long range projects and activities

1. *Future Paper.* Have students write a newspaper from the viewpoint and knowledge of people living at some point in the future. The various columns—weather, sports, local news—should reflect life as it is in that time.

2. *Class Magazine.* Select a theme, give the magazine a title, choose the various sections and articles, discuss who the magazine's readers will be—parents, younger students, peers. You might want to use the magazine as a fund-raising activity—sell subscriptions, get advertisers.

3. *Class Anthology.* Select examples of the best writing done over a period of time and include them in a class anthology. You can get a copy professionally bound—it is less expensive than you might think—or bind it yourself with the help of your class.

4. *Build a Creative-Writing Section or Space.* Work with the students to select a classroom space, perhaps an entire corner or area. Add ideas to an idea box; create displays of books, students' writings, motivational ideas; get a rug and furniture; design the environment with aesthetics and practicality in mind; provide tools—paper, pencil, checklists, and charts for various activities, such as "How To Proofread," "How To Evaluate Your Story"; create ways to share what has been written—a bulletin-board display, tape recordings of the students reading their poetry.

miscellaneous ideas

1. Give students a precise number of words to write in a particular writing activity—write either seventeen, thirty-seven, or fifty-seven words on "If I Weren't _____."

2. Provide a special creative time, every day, every other day, or every week; have a creative time at different times each day or week. Decide what works best for you and your students.

3. Have students prepare a "radio" show every morning, or however often is best. Students can tape record the show with regular features (this could be recorded the day before or on the morning of the show). Students could write different features for the show, like a continuing serial, a critic's corner, or whatever interests them.

4. Talk with other teachers; observe what they do for creative writing. Many ideas can be shared. Talk with your students about what they've done in other classes; it might spark new ideas.

5. Create writing contests of all kinds: the funniest poem, the best descriptive story, the best argumentative essay.

6. Have students, and yourself, keep a note pad handy for new words, story ideas, thoughts they hear, unusual quotes, things they observe. These can be used in future writing activities.

7. Invite writers to speak and read their work to your class. I had a friend, a poet, who spoke to my class about writing. He asked them to write something for him, which they all did. He took their work home and wrote a personal response to each student. His visit to the class and comments to each student helped motivate a torrent of creative writing.

8. Create a club—call it the Writer's Circle, or whatever—for students interested in creative writing. Give them their own space and time to meet. Your placing value and importance on the club will help motivate others to join.

9. Have a beautifully decorated box available for all written work students wish to share with you. Have them label their work as follows:

"A," If they want just you to read it;

"B," If they want to share it with the class;

"C" If they would like to meet with you to discuss and improve their creation.

10. Have students use pen names—for anonymity and/or fun.

practical uses

1. Have each student write an autobiography in preparation for filling out a personal resume or a job application.

2. Have students write to pen pals.

3. Have students write a neighborhood guide: where to go, what to do; review stores and facilities in the neighborhood; interview people of interest in the community; supply important information—dangerous things to avoid in the area, what time stores close.

4. Have students write letters to specific organizations or individuals for specific purposes—letters to the editor of a magazine or newspaper, requests for a photograph from a star, a complaint or compliment to a manufacturer.

5. Have each student write a satire about an existing situation, using the satire to motivate for change.

6. Have students create cards for all kinds of occasions and reasons—for a sick classmate, friend or family member; for holidays, birthdays, giving thanks.

curriculum areas

See Chapter 8 for additional ideas.

1. Have students take a time-capsule ride to the past. Write about the experience, discussing the people, places, and things as they existed at that time. Take a ride to the future, and base what is written on the scientific truths and principles studied in class.

2. Have the students write a textbook on a subject area. The students will be given responsibility for different topics in the subject.

3. Have students prepare a play based on subjects studied; for example, after studying the Civil War, a short series of skits can be written by groups of students.

writing-skill development

Have students:

1. Analyze the writing about the main character in a story: name and synonyms used to describe the protagonist; adjectives and synonyms used to describe the protagonist; participles or verbs and synonyms used to describe the actions of the protagonist; persons, places or things related to the protagonist. Using one word from each category, write a sentence describing the protagonist's character and responses.

2. Brainstorm by bringing in various objects and asking students for ways the object can be used; list the ideas with no discussion—you can have students do this by groups. Write an essay or story based on the ideas presented during the brainstorming.

3. Write a story whose every sentence begins with a descriptive word.

using other art forms

1. Have someone good in art draw a picture every day. Each student can write a story or thought based on his reaction to the drawing.

2. Have each student draw the shape of any object in an exaggerated form, then write a story or poem inside that shape.

3. Have students listen to music and write a story, poem, words, or whatever comes to mind based on the music's inspiration.

4. Use a picture or photograph and have students write stories telling what led up to and what followed the scene shown; write poems on the feelings inspired; write humorous captions. The picture or photographs would be selected based on the specific writing activity to be developed. A photograph or picture can be selected to illustrate a poem or story already written.

5. Have students write poetry or a narration for a choral speaking program.

6. Have the class observe a ballet or other form of dance and write a story or poem based on that dance; write a poem or story and create a dance based on what was written.

7. Have students write the lyrics to a melody.

8. Have each student write an expository essay explaining how to create in an art form, such as how to take good photographs.

observation

1. Ask questions that focus students' attention on what they observe with their senses or the ways they use their senses: What color are your parents' eyes? What are the most unusual sounds you hear outside your house? What is the worst thing you ever smelled? What is the sourest thing you ever ate? What things cause you to itch?

2. Help students focus attention on their environment using different senses: List five things you've never observed (with any sense or a particular sense) in the classroom, your home, or the street near your home; observe using only one sense and try to eliminate other senses—cover your eyes and listen for a particular sound, cover your ears and try to figure out what two people are discussing, close your eyes and smell or taste some food.

3. Have students secretly observe another student during lunch. List the things observed and share them with the one observed.

4. Arrange to have a student unknown to the class suddenly storm into the classroom. Have him shout something and create some kind of disturbance so everyone in your class will pay attention to him; then have him leave very quickly. Have the class write up the incident: What did he look like? What was the first thing he did? Tell them you will have to send their report to the principal. After they've finished writing, bring the student back into the room and have your class compare what they wrote about him and what he did with what he actually looks like and actually did. Discuss the activity with your class.

5. Assign various students to look for or create things for the class to observe: when walking on a trip, assign one student to yell "stop" and point out some specific thing for everyone to observe, then have another student yell out the next time—you can give students categories of things to look for, like a colorful scene, a pleasant sound, an ugly sight, a funny feeling thing.

6. Have students listen or watch for the auditory or visual rhythms that exist in the environment: the regular movement of a water sprinkler, a flag blowing in the wind, the sound of traffic going over a bump in the street.

vocabulary development

1. Help your students use and be around words as much as possible:

> Read
> Talk
> Listen
> Discuss
> Write

2. Have students use the tools of a writer—a dictionary, a thesaurus; have the students make their own thesaurus and dictionary.

3. Have a display or file of word categories. As students find words that belong in each category, they can add to the list or file.

4. Stress to the students that they should use new words they learn as soon and as often as possible.

5. Introduce new words in all your activities with your students. Don't underestimate their ability to learn and understand new vocabulary: instead of "fear," say "trepidation"; be sure your students learn the meaning of any new words you use.

6. Introduce particularly long or unusual words. Students will enjoy learning and using these: "syzygy," "antidisestablishmentarianism," "serendipity."

7. Have the student keep a notebook or index cards with new words. Use categories of words—sounds, feelings, motions, places, ₋nimals.

8. Introduce suffixes and prefixes, demonstrating how they change the meaning of root words to which they are added.

9. "Vocabulary bees" can be used in the manner of spelling bees. Ask for the definition of a word and have the student use it in a meaningful sentence. A variation can be to give the definition and have the student give the word.

poetry

1. Have students listen for poetry in radio and TV commercials.

2. Have students make up new lyrics for their favorite songs.

3. Have students change a couple of lines of popular poems, keeping the same rhythm and rhyming pattern.

4. Find a picture or photograph that appeals to a student's sense of imagery. Have the student use similes or metaphors to describe the scene.

5. Have students write poetic commercials for products.

6. Have students write poems they know will be read to others or recorded for others to hear.

non-fiction (essay)

Have students:

1. Make up "wanted" posters for autobiographies; describe the physical and personal characteristics of the writer.

2. Make up riddles and jokes.

3. Write an ad describing a product and convincing someone to buy a product.

4. Write an advice column.

5. Write editorials about something happening in school and present it to the appropriate person.

6. Write a manual of instruction on "How to __(a topic of interest)__ ."

7. Hold a debate on a topic of controversy with the students writing their viewpoints before debating the topic.

fiction

1. Ways to help stimulate story writing:

Start with titles to stimulate story writing—let a group of students help you make a list of story titles;

present an opening paragraph, a picture, the last line of a story—The boys never battled each other again;

look at a picture, photograph, visual scene in the environment—an elderly couple walking hand in hand, firemen putting out a fire, a group of street dogs.

2. Have students brainstorm for story ideas and then brainstorm for the story elements based on that idea.

3. Have the class create stories that exaggerate everything and everyone in it.

4. Have students create myths about something that disturbs or upsets them: why we have scary thoughts, when people learned to yell.

evaluating and editing

1. Have students edit and evaluate the papers of other students, looking for and commenting only on the things they feel are good and correct.

2. Have students evaluate their papers for what they really like about them, listing the good points.

3. Present written samples before revision and after revision; let the content be of interest to students.

4. Let students edit their papers and decide in what skill areas they need and want help.

5. Give, or let each student write, a checklist of things to look for when editing. The list could be as general or specific as appropriate.

6. Take one particularly good story written by a student and have a copy made for everyone in class. Let everyone circle what they liked in the story.

7. Take a story written by a student and, with her agreement, ditto the work for everyone in class, or use an opaque projector, or make an overhead projection. Have the class edit for mistakes.

8. Form an editing committee to select work for a class publication, indicating to the writer how they want the work edited for the magazine. Discuss the responsibilities of an editor with the entire class—the editors should have the right to decide what they want in a publication and how it should be written.

9. Hold regular conferences with each student, discussing whatever is relevant and appropriate.

sharing and displaying

1. Find publications to which students can submit written work (see Resources).

2. Create an art festival at which students' work can be displayed.

3. Display written work anonymously, with the class to guess who wrote the material.

4. Create a "coffeehouse" environment and have the students read their work aloud.

5. Have students sell subscriptions to a class magazine as a fundraiser, with students' creative writing included in the publication.

6. Have a special time and place when and where writers can share their creations with others.

7. Have writers share their work with other classes—use a roving display board that can go from class to class, have students read written material to another class.

8. Put a large piece of paper on a display board or wall. Have students use the paper to write their personal thoughts and quotes they would like to share.

glossary

Allegory A story with an underlying meaning, different from the obvious, surface, or apparent meaning. It can be read, or written, at different levels: 1) Reacting to the surface story; 2) Looking for the theme being communicated by the story; 3) Deciding who or what the story characters, places, or events represent in the real world.

Alliteration The regular repetition of consonant and/or vowel sounds; the *b*ig *b*ad *b*oy *b*it the *b*ad *b*anana; *o*pen to the *o*nly *o*de he wrote.

Allusion An indirect reference to something, using a metaphor.

Analogy A comparison of things, showing a similarity between things that are unlike in other ways—comparing a computer to the human brain.

Anapestic Having to do with the measure or "foot" in poetry consisting of two unaccented syllables followed by an accented one, or two short syllables followed by a long one: I have cóme/ to the séa.

Anecdote A short narrative of an interesting incident or event.

Anthology   A collection of poetry or prose selections, either by the same author or various authors.

Anthropomorphic   To attribute human characteristics to gods, non-human beings, or things: The tree was crying.

Antithesis   The placing of two sharply contrasting ideas in adjoining sentences or next to each other in one sentence: "Give me liberty or give me death." or "To err is human; to forgive, divine."

Antonym   A word having the opposite meaning of another word; "hot" is the antonym for "cold."

Aphorism   A concise statement that expresses a general thought or truth: "A bird in the hand is worth two in the bush."

Argumentative essay   This essay attempts to persuade or convince the reader to accept an idea, viewpoint, attitude, or belief. Attention is given to illustrating the truth or falsehood of something. The purpose of the writer is to motivate the reader to do something.

Assonance   Rhyme in which the same vowel sounds are used with different consonants—lame, train; beat, mean.

Autonomasia   Using the name of a person, usually well-known, as a substitute for the name of another person having similar characteristics: instead of saying "Here comes Pete," say "Here comes Don Juan."

Blank verse   Unrhymed poetry or verses; especially unrhymed poetry having five iambic feet in each line (iambic pentameter).

Brainstorming   A technique for solving problems, building information, stimulating creative thinking, or developing new ideas, in which one or more persons spontaneously and unrestrainedly calls out or in some way presents information, ideas, viewpoints.

Cadence   The rhythmic flow or pattern of words in poetry or prose.

Caesura   A pause in a line of poetry, usually occurring where the pause is required by the sense or natural speech rhythms.

Caption   The title or heading at the top of a page, article, chapter, or under a picture, explaining it.

Characterization   The development and description of the qualities, features, and personality of characters in a story or play.

Cinquain   A five-line poem with the following word or syllable pattern:

1st line, one word (or two syllables)—gives title
2nd line, two words (or four syllables)—describes title
3rd line, three words (or six syllables)—expresses action
4th line, four words (or eight syllables)—expresses a feeling
5th line, one word (or two syllables)—another word for the title.

An example of a cinquain is as follows:

Dancer
graceful, artistic
glides, spins, leaps
Joy, pride, exhilarate, tender
Ballerina

Cliche   An idea or expression that has lost originality or impact by overuse: "sadder but wiser"; "strong as an ox."

Comparison   Finding likenesses or differences between things; similes, metaphors, and analogies are types of comparisons.

Couplet   The simplest form of rhymed verse. It has two lines, each with the same, or approximately the same, number of syllables and with rhyming end words:

The four-year-old flows her dancing body through the air,
The audience marvels at her poetry of motion—and stare.

Creative writing   An artistic tool for expression through a particular style and form of writing, personal feelings, beliefs, ideas, and information; it's a written creation intended by the writer to create some type of impression and have some kind of emotional, intellectual, or spiritual effect on the reader.

Criticism   The act of making judgments or evaluations; the determination of the goodness or badness, rightness or wrongness of something; the reasons something is good or bad, right or wrong.

Deduction   Going from generalization to specifics; presents the conclusion first (the point to be proved), then gives the evidence that supports that conclusion.

Description   Writing that describes; it creates pictures with words, conveying an image or impression that shows the appearance, nature, and qualities of the thing described.

Descriptive essay   Reveals or suggests a picture, the physical appearance of some person, place, or thing. It tries to create a picture, or image, in the reader's mind.

Dialogue   Conversation between characters in a literary work; what a character says and how he speaks.

Diamente   A structured form of writing that has seven lines and contains a contrast (a comparison that shows a difference between things); its pattern is:

1st line, a noun that names an object or thought;

2nd line, two adjectives that describe the noun;

3rd line, three participles (-ing, or -ed words) that relate to the noun;

4th line, four nouns, two referring to the noun in line 1, two referring to the noun in line 7;

5th line, three participles that relate to the noun in line 7;

6th line, two adjectives that describe the noun in line 7;

7th line, a noun that names an object or thought that is opposite the noun in line 1.

For example:

PLAYER
swift, agile
running, hustling, competing
pride, fulfillment, numbness, dissatisfaction
sitting, watching, bored
lazy, motionless
SPECTATOR

Diction   The choice and use of words by the writer.

Editing   The process through which the editor adds, omits, changes, or makes no changes, to a written creation.

Editorial   An article in a magazine or newspaper (or statement in the broadcast media) by the editor, or under his direction, giving an opinion regarding some subject.

Epic poem   A long narrative poem that tells of the adventures of one or more great heroes; it's written in a majestic, elevated style.

Epigram   A concise, incisive, or witty saying: "May the best be the worst you know"; a short poem ending in a witty or clever turn of thought:

> *A wise old owl lived in an oak.*
> *The more he saw, the less he spoke.*
> *The less he spoke, the more he heard.*
> *Why can't we all be like that bird?*

Episode   An incident, event, or scene in a novel or story that is usually fully developed and can be integrated into the main plot or digress from it.

Epithet   A descriptive word or phrase expressing some quality or attribute of some person or thing: "brilliant John" ("brilliant" is the epithet); "Richard the Lion-Hearted" ("Lion-Hearted" is the epithet).

Essay   A short literary composition that can explain, describe, persuade, or tell a story about a particular subject or theme.

Euphemism   A mild or indirect term or expression instead of one that is harsh or unpleasantly direct: "sanitary engineer" is a euphemism for "garbage man."

Evaluation   Determining the value of something; examining and judging.

Expository essay   This essay explains or conveys facts and ideas. It's written in a clear, definite format.

Fable   A fictitious story, often with and about animals or inanimate objects who speak; its purpose is to teach a moral (a principle for right conduct and survival).

Fairy tale   A story, usually for a child, about magical creatures (elves, fairies, dragons, witches) involving legendary deeds and romance.

Fantasy   An imaginative or fanciful work, especially one that deals with supernatural or unnatural events and characters.

Fiction   Writing that employs imaginary characters, events, and settings created by the writer.

Figure of speech   An expression in which words are used in other than their literal sense or in unusual combinations, usually to make a comparison between two unlike things; similes, metaphors, personifications are figures of speech.

Flashback   An interruption in a story to portray or recount an incident or event from the past.

Folk tale   A tale or legend passed down from generation to generation among a people or group.

Foot   A group of stressed and unstressed syllables forming a metrical unit of a verse: in "undér/ the cháir/ he found/ the báll," "undér"/ forms a metrical unit. There are four feet (tetrameter) to this line of verse.

Formal essay   This essay focuses on the subject, which is presented in a straightforward, conventional style of writing.

Free verse   Poetry not restricted by the usual rules about meter and rhyme.

Haiku   A Japanese poem of three lines, having a total of seventeen syllables; the line pattern is:

1st line, five syllables;

2nd line, seven syllables;

3rd line, five syllables.

Its theme is generally about nature:

> *I look at the wind,*
> *I see it bend the young trees,*
> *As their parents watch.*

Iamb   This is the metrical unit in a line of verse that has the common rhythm of an unstressed syllable followed by a stressed syllable: in "I síng/ to yóu," "I síng" is an iambic foot and "to yóu" is an iambic foot.

Idiom   A phrase or expression whose meaning cannot be understood from the usual meanings of the words: "kick the bucket," "I am under the weather."

Imagery   Creating vivid descriptions and sensory pictures with words.

Induction   Going from specifics to generalizations; first presenting the specific facts, ideas, and observations and drawing a conclusion (generalization) based on them.

Informal essay   This essay is a free-form style of writing. What comes through is the writer's personality.

Irony   An expression that says the opposite of what is really intended: "Hey, fatty" said to a very skinny person; "It sure is beautiful," during a miserable streak of weather.

Legend   An unhistorical or unverifiable story handed down by tradition from early times, and popularly accepted as historical; it denotes a fictitious story, usually concerned with a real person, place, or other subject, and sometimes involves the supernatural.

Limerick   A popular form of nonsense verse. There are five lines. The rhyming pattern is 1-1-2-2-1, with three beats in lines 1, 2, and 5, and two beats for lines 3 and 4. In lines 1, 2, and 5, the stress is on the second, fifth, and eighth syllables.

The poem is in reality two poems—a three-line poem (lines 1, 2, and 5), and a two-line poem (lines 3 and 4).

Line 5 usually ends with humor or a surprise. The poet can use crazy spelling and unusual twists and have a creative, imaginative ball.

> *There is a boy whose name is Lou*
> *He loved to be with you-know-who.*
> *He kissed her nose,*
> *Stepped on her toes,*
> *And on his shin he felt her shoe.*

Litotes   An understatement; the opposite of exaggeration: "a million dollars is no small amount"; "not bad at all."

Lyric poem   A short poem expressing personal emotions—a love poem, a lament, a hymn (song of praise).

Manuscript   The author's copy of his work that is prepared and submitted for publication.

Maxim   A statement of general truth; a short rule of conduct: "Think before you act," "Look before you leap."

Metaphor   An indirect form of comparing things, without using "like" or "as": "Easter is glorious hats, painted eggs, and hopping rabbits"; "he is an iceberg under conditions of turmoil."

Meter   Poetic rhythm; the arrangements of beats and accents in a line of poetry (see *foot* and *iamb*).

Metonymy   Use of the name of one thing to suggest something else: "canvas" instead of "sails"; "count heads" for "count the number of people."

Muse   One of the nine Greek goddesses of the fine arts; the spirit that inspires an artist.

Myth   A type of story that usually concerns gods, godlike heroes, or heroes bigger than life; its purpose is to try to explain some belief or natural event.

Narrative   This is the general term for any story, long or short, factual or imagined, past, present, or future. It can be told for any purpose, with or without much detail.

Narrative essay   This essay tells a story or presents a series of events in the order they occur. Its purpose is to give meaning to an event or a series of events by telling a story.

Novel   A fictitious prose narrative of considerable length, setting and presenting the action in the form of a plot.

Ode   A lyric poem having an exalted style (noble feeling expressed with dignity).

Onomatopoeia   A word that sounds like that to which it refers: the *buzz* of a bee; the *hiss* of a snake.

Palindrome   A word, line, or verse that reads the same forward and backward: "Otto"; "Madam, I'm Adam."

Pantoum   A verse form from Malay, consisting of quatrains in which the second and fourth lines are repeated as the first and third lines of the following quatrain; the final line of the poem can repeat the opening line.

The people all run
As the storm comes near
They look with wonder
They shout with fear

As the storm comes near
The people feel helpless
They shout with fear
Faces contort in distress

The people feel helpless
The storm has begun
Faces contort with distress
The people all run

Parable A short story used to teach some truth or moral lesson.

Parody A humorous imitation of a serious piece of writing.

Personification Gives personal human qualities to inanimate objects; the tree felt lonely; the clouds roared with anger.

Plot The organization and presentation of the story's events and situations; the plan and design of a story.

Poetic license Liberty taken by a prose writer or poet in varying from the accepted rules, forms, facts, and usages.

Poetry (See Chapter 6)

Portmanteau word A word made by putting together parts of other words; these words convey an effect and show meaning by echoing one or more familiar words: "smog" from "smoke" and "fog."

Proofread Reading to detect errors for correction.

Prose The ordinary form of speech and writing, without metrical structure, as differentiated from verse.

Protagonist A leading character in a novel, story, or play.

Quatrain A poem or stanza of four lines with any of the following rhyme schemes: abcb, abab, abba (generally the second and fourth lines have rhyming end words—"abcb" pattern):

Roses are red
Violets are blue

> *Sugar is sweet*
> *And I love you.*

Revise   To change, modify, and improve as needed and appropriate.

Rhyme   One word agreeing with, sounding like another in the final sound:

> *He dropped the* meat,
> *Upon his* feet.

Rhythm   The flow and movement of sound; it's influenced by the repetition of words, phrases, ideas, and silences; the steady repeating pattern of stressed and unstressed syllables is what basically determines the rhythmic flow of a poem.

Satire   A poem, essay, story that ridicules or holds up to scorn habits, customs, and ideas.

Senryu   A Japanese poem similar to haiku, generally concerned with human nature, but usually humorous and not necessarily keeping to the syllable requirements of haiku.

> *I look in the mirror,*
> *I am again slim and trim.*
> *Then my eyes open.*

Serial   Anything published or broadcast in installments.

Setting   The locale and time period of a story; the background in which the story takes place and including the physical, social, emotional, mental, or spiritual environment of the story.

Sextet   Six-line verse with many possible variations of rhyme, line length, and rhythm; the last six lines of a sonnet.

Short story   A piece of prose fiction, usually under 10,000 words (see Chapter 7).

Simile   A comparison of things using "like" or "as": "She runs like a cheetah"; "He looked like a concave lens."

Sonnet   A fourteen-line poem in iambic pentameter (a pentameter is a line of poetry having five feet; see *iamb* and *foot*). It embodies the statement and resolution of a single theme, thought, or sentiment: rhyming schemes can vary.

Stanza   A group of lines of a poem, generally four or more, arranged according to a fixed plan.

Style   The way the writer puts down the words he has chosen to use; the form of expression as opposed to the content of the thought expressed.

Synecdoche   A figure of speech in which a more inclusive term is used for a less inclusive term or vice versa: *law* for *policeman*.

Synonym   A word having the same or nearly the same meaning as another word: *skinny* and *slim*; *finish* and *complete*.

Tanka   A Japanese poem concentrating on nature, having a total of thirty-one syllables; the first and third lines have five syllables, the second, fourth and fifth lines have seven syllables.

> *I breathe the clean air,*
> *It seems to cleanse my body.*
> *It refreshes me.*
> *What a glorious pleasure,*
> *To feel my body rejoice.*

Theme   The writer's sense of what the main concept or viewpoint is that's presented in the story or poem.

Tragedy   A literary work that deals with a serious, gloomy, somber theme, with a tragic conclusion.

Transition   The bridge that joins parts of the composition, and helps clarify the relationships of different parts of the essay or story, e.g., later, in addition, however; etc.

Trite word or expression   A word or expression that is no longer fresh, or interesting; worn out by use, stale.

Trope   Any word used in a sense different from its ordinary meaning; e.g., metaphors, metonymy, etc.

Verse   A single metrical line of a poem; a stanza of a poem.

Yarn   A tale; a long story of adventure or incredible happenings.

resources

A resource is an available supply on which you can draw; it is as valuable as it is appropriate to your creative-writing program and your needs, interests, and purposes. The following list of resources is intended to present ideas and information that will direct your attention and efforts to find other possible resources that are relevant to your creative writing program

people

Fellow teachers, educators (including administrative and supervisory personnel), and students can be most helpful. Pick their brains for ideas, observe what they are doing or have done, share your thoughts with them and get their feedback. Don't overlook your students; they have a wealth of ideas and information on books, activities, and projects.

Writers can be brought in to help motivate your students, direct their attention and creative energy, and help develop their attitudes, understandings, and skills as writers. Writers are available from many sources: your friends and acquaintances, friends of friends, through various funded programs (see "Artists in the Schools"), successful student writers.

You can write, or have your students write, successful authors for information and advice on writing. If you don't know or have access to a writer's address, write to them in care of the publisher of his or her latest book.

Librarians (children's and adults') are paid to help people find books and information. They can be of tremendous help in directing you to the proper sources and resources.

organizations

Teachers & Writers Collaborative
84 Fifth Ave.
New York, N.Y. 10011

This organization provides a wealth of information and ideas on and for creative writing. The organization sends writers (and other artists) into New York City public schools to work with teachers and students in conducting long-term projects. It publishes or distributes a variety of books and material, including a magazine that comes out three times a year.

National Council of Teachers of English (NCTE)
1111 Kenyon Rd.
Urbana, Ill. 61801

This organization publishes (or published) various material that will be most helpful:

Language Arts (formerly *Elementary English*) is published eight times during the school year and covers elementary language-arts programs and curriculum, including creative writing.

English Journal, published nine times a year, for middle-school, junior- and senior-high-school teachers. It includes articles on creative writing.

NCTE Catalogue: Professional Publications for the Teacher of English and the Language Arts.   This is an annual catalogue that lists all material published or distributed by NCTE. Sections on "Compo-

sition" and "Ideas for the Classroom" list publications that deal with creative writing.

Creative Writing in the Classroom: An Annotated Bibliography of Selected Resources (K-12), Robert Day, Editor. This is truly an *invaluable* resource. It annotates over 700 books and articles published between 1950 and 1976 that are concerned with the theory and practice of creative writing for elementary and secondary teachers and students. It is a wonderful aid to help teachers locate a variety of materials that give ideas, information, and special resources (supplementary materials, student anthologies, reference aids, and other aids to use in creative writing).

artists in the schools programs

These programs involve professional writers working with students in classrooms. These artists can be a priceless resource. You can find out about local programs by contacting your state arts council (*A Dictionary of American Fiction Writers*—available from NCTE—provides addresses of state arts councils).

magazines for teachers

The following magazines have articles that cover the theory and practice of creative writing. You can find ideas and information that apply to your needs and interests, including specific activities to do with and for your students.

American Education
Childhood Education
Elementary School Journal
English Journal
Instructor
Language Arts (formerly *Elementary English*)
Learning

Media and Methods
Reading Teacher
Teacher (formerly *Grade Teacher*)

The Educational Index, the ERIC (Educational Resources Information Center) Index System, and CIJE (Current Index to Journals in Education, published in cooperation with ERIC), are excellent sources for locating information on creative writing. These should be available at any major library. *Ulrich's International Periodicals Dictionary* (a Bowker Serials Bibliography) lists magazines under appropriate topic headings. You can locate a specific magazine that would be relevant for a particular need, interest, or purpose, that either you or a student may have (it lists magazines for children and youths). Most libraries will have this available.

magazines for students

(See *Ulrich's International Periodicals Directory*)

magazines that publish student's work

Even though only a small percentage of submitted work is actually published (a fact of which your students should be made aware), the possibility of having something published in a magazine can be a wonderful motivation and creates a meaningful purpose for a writer.

Write to individual magazines for their policies on accepting student writing, because their policies are subject to change. In general, include the name, age, grade level, and address of the student; include a note signed by a parent or teacher that verifies that the work is original; be sure the submission is very legible (typing it double spaced is best); if you wish the work returned, include a self-addressed, stamped envelope.

American Girl,
830 Third Ave.,
New York, N.Y. 10022

For girls twelve to seventeen. Accepts stories, poetry, art, and letters.

Child Life,
1100 Waterway Blvd.,
P.O. Box 567B,
Indianapolis, Ind. 46206

Science fiction and mystery magazine for children seven to eleven. Accepts letters, poems, art, and short stories with a mystery or science fiction theme.

Children's Playmate (same address as **Child Life**)

For children three to eight. Accepts stories, art, jokes, riddles, and poetry.

Cricket,
Open Court Publishing Company,
P.O. Box 599,
LaSalle, Ill. 61301

For children five to twelve. Accepts letters and riddles; holds monthly contests for stories, poetry, and art based on a given theme. It may publish other work by children.

Daisy,
830 Third Ave.,
New York, N.Y. 10022

For children six to eleven. It accepts stories, poems, descriptions of craft projects, and activities and puzzles.

Ebony Jr!,
820 S. Michigan Ave.,
Chicago, Ill 60605

For children six to twelve. Accepts letters, news of children's achievements, art, poetry, stories, and cartoon strips. Writing contests are held annually. No work will be returned.

166   resources

Highlights for Children,
2300 W. Fifth Ave.,
P.O. Box 269,
Columbus, Ohio 43216

For children three to twelve. Accepts letters, jokes, stories, poetry, art, riddles.

Jack and Jill (same address as **Child Life**)

For children ages eight to twelve. Accepts letters, poems, art photos of children, and short stories.

Ranger Rick's Nature Magazine,
1412 Sixteenth St. N.W.,
Washington, D.C. 20036

For children five to twelve years old. Accepts poems and art on nature subjects. Materials cannot be returned.

Read Magazine,
Xerox Education Publications,
Education Center,
Columbus, Ohio 43216

For grades seven to nine. Regularly includes students' jokes and poetry. Once a year has a special student issue devoted to poetry, short stories, plays, and other types of writing by students.

Scholastic Scope,
50 W. 44th Street,
New York, N.Y. 10036

For grades seven through twelve (directed to students who read at fourth- to sixth-grade level). Publishes poems, stories, plays, and "mini-mysteries." Entries should be sent in care of "Student Writing" or "Mini Mysteries." A note verifying the originality of the work must be signed by the student *and* a parent or teacher.

Scholastic Voice, Scholastic Magazines Inc. (same address as Scholastic Scope)

For grades nine through twelve. Publishes poems and stories of less than 500 words. Features regular writing contests on themes. Entries should be sent to "Your Turn," and a note signed by the student *and* a parent or teacher verifying the originality of the work must be submitted.

Seventeen,
850 Third Ave.,
New York, N.Y. 10022

For teen-agers, especially girls. Accepts original short fiction, poetry, mood pieces, opinion columns, and articles about personal experiences. Sponsors an annual fiction contest for boys and girls aged thirteen through nineteen; prizes and honorable mentions are awarded, and winners' work is published in *Seventeen.* Contest rules are announced in a spring issue of the magazine.

Stone Soup,
Box 83,
Santa Cruz, Calif. 95063

For children four to twelve. It's written and illustrated entirely by children.

Wee Wisdom,
Unity Village, Mo. 64065

An educational and "character-building" magazine for children three to twelve. Accepts stories and poems. The August/September issue features children's work exclusively.

Weewish Tree,
American Indian Historical Society,
1451 Masonic Ave.,
San Francisco, Calif. 94117

For elementary through secondary level, accepts stories, poetry, and art with American Indian related themes.

Young World,
Saturday Evening Post Company,
1100 Waterway Blvd.,
P.O. Box 567B,
Indianapolis, Ind. 46206

For ages ten to fourteen. Accepts letters, poetry, stories, articles, art, and jokes.

writing contests

Contests can be a source of motivation and help create a meaningful purpose for students to write. Entering a contest should be seen and approached with enjoyment; be careful to prevent its becoming a pressured activity that would cause upset beyond disappointment and result in a student's feeling invalidated if he or she does not win.

The following magazines and organizations sponsor contests. Write to them for further information. In addition, there are many local writing contests sponsored by various organizations; be on the lookout for those.

Ebony Jr!, Cricket, Seventeen, and *Scholastic Voice* have been mentioned earlier; they all sponsor writing contests.

English Journal,
Spring Poetry Festival,
P.O. Box 112,
East Lansing, Mich. 48823

Each May, *English Journal* features a poetry festival. Rules for submission are included in an autumn issue each year.

Know Your World,
Xerox Education Publications,
245 Long Hill Rd.,
Middletown, Conn. 06457

For ten- to sixteen-year-olds who read at the second- to third-grade level. Once a year the magazine sponsors a story ending contest. Rules are included in the teachers' addition.

NCTE Achievement Awards in Writing,
National Council of Teachers of English,
1111 Kenyon Road,
Urbana, Ill. 61801

Each year, eight hundred achievement awards are presented to high school students. To be eligible, a high school junior must be nominated by his or her high school English department. Contestants are judged on the basis of two compositions: an impromptu theme on a given topic, written under a teacher's supervision; and a writing sample of their choice, either poetry, fiction, or non-fiction. Write the NCTE Director of Achievement Awards for more information.

Scholastic Magazines Writing Awards,
50 W. 44th St.,
New York, N.Y. 10036

For students in grades seven through twelve, who may submit short stories, poetry, drama, and articles. Certificates, cash prizes, and scholarships are awarded to winners, whose entries are published in many Scholastic Magazines publications, including *Scholastic Scope, Scholastic Voice,* and *Literary Cavalcade.* Entry blanks are included in the December issue of *Literary Cavalcade* each year and may be obtained from Scholastic Magazines after Oct. 1 each year.

Weekly Reader (same address as **Know Your World**).

Senior Weekly Reader (for sixth-graders) sponsors story ending contests. Occasionally, the fourth- and fifth-grade editions of *Weekly Reader* sponsor story and poetry ending contests.

You and Your World (same address as **Know Your World**).

For students ages fourteen through eighteen and older who read at a third- to fifth-grade level. Once a year the magazine sponsors a story ending contest. Rules are included in the teachers' edition.

books

Books are a very effective tool for getting children interested, motivated, and learning about creative writing. However, there is an incredible quantity of books for children to choose from. The following resources should help you select the material that best suits your needs, interests, and purposes.

lists and annotated bibliographies

There are many lists and publications that annotate books for children (students). They are an excellent source to help you find appropriate material to read to pre-school through teen-age students or to be read by them. I will list a few of these; a children's library should have many others.

Let's Read Together,
American Library Association,
50 E. Huron St.,
Chicago, Ill 60611

This is an annotated list of books organized by interests as well as age level; it includes brief descriptions and specific recommendations.

Carlson, Ruth Kearney, *Enrichment Ideas.* Dubuque, Iowa: Wm. C. Brown, 1970.

This book is filled with ideas and suggestions for using literature to enrich various areas of the curriculum, including creative writing. Specific books are recommended appropriate to the subject matter discussed.

Larrick, Nancy, *A Parent's Guide To Children's Reading.* New York: Doubleday, 1975.

Nearly 700 titles are annotated for content and age level; it includes discussion of how to best use literature to develop children's interest and ability to read.

Sutherland, Zena, and Mary Hill Arbuthnot, *Children and Books,* fifth
   edition. Glenview, Ill.: Scott, Foresman, 1977.

An extensive and comprehensive book; it discusses books, authors,
   and children and includes book selection aids, references, publisher's addresses, and other information and advice that will
   prove helpful.

book publisher catalogues

You can send away to the various publishers of children's books
and request their catalogues.

Scholastic Book Services is an excellent source of paperbacks for
   K-12 students. Send for *Reader's Choice Paperback Catalogue,*
   a complete and descriptive list of titles. Write to:
   > Scholastic Book Services
   > 904 Sylvan Ave.
   > Englewood Cliffs, N.J. 07632

In addition, you can: use librarians for information; browse
through bookstores and libraries; have your students create and share
their own books and anthologies; ask your students to bring and share
their books; and exchange books with other classes.

some recommended anthologies
of children's writing

**Here I Am! An Anthology of Poems Written by Young People in Some of
   America's Minority Groups,** ed. Virginia Olsen Baron. New York:
   Dutton, 1969. (Also available from Bantam in paperback)

Poems of children and teen-agers of minority groups including black,
   Puerto Rican, Japanese, Chinese, and American Indian.

Mad, Sad & Glad, ed. Stephen Dunning. Scholastic Book Services,
   1970.

Poems of winners from Scholastic Magazines' creative-writing contests, for students in grades seven through twelve.

The Me Nobody Knows: Children's Voices From the Ghetto, ed. Stephen M. Joseph. Avon Books, 1969.

Poetry and prose from mainly black and Puerto Rican children, ages seven through eighteen. It's about growing up in the ghettos of New York City.

How Children See Our World, ed. Jella Lepman. Avon Books, 1971.

A collection of writings and drawings expressing the thoughts of children from 35 countries on a wide variety of topics.

Miracles: Poems by Children of the English-Speaking World, ed. Richard Lewis. New York: Simon & Schuster, 1966.

Nearly 200 poems by children from the United States, England, New Zealand, Kenya, Uganda, Australia, India, and the Philippines.

Journey: Prose by Children of the English-Speaking World, ed. Richard Lewis. New York: Simon & Schuster, 1969.

A companion to *Miracles,* covers a wide variety of topics.

Marshall, Eric, and Stuart Hample. *Children's Letters To God.* Collins Publishers, 1975.

Actual letters written by children covering a wide gamut of thoughts and wishes.

How To Grow A Child: A Child's Advice To Parents, ed. Bernard Percy. Los Angeles: Price, Stern & Sloan Publishers, Inc., 1978.

Students, ages ten through fourteen, communicate their insights and viewpoints on raising children.

resource books for teachers of creative writing

Books on creative writing can provide inspiration, motivation, ideas, techniques, advice, philosophy, information, guidance, examples, and methodology.

The following book list may prove helpful, but I again refer you to the book put out by NCTE, *Creative Writing in the Classroom: An Annotated Bibliography of Selected Resources (K–12)*, ed. Robert Day. You will probably be able to find a book or article mentioned that will more than likely meet your specific needs, interests, and purposes.

Blake, Jim and Barbara Ernst. *The Great Perpetual Learning Machine.* Boston: Little, Brown, 1976.

A book filled with ideas, games, experiments, and activities, to help students experience the world around them and create opportunities, ideas, and motivation to write. Many resource books are mentioned and discussed throughout the book.

Bogojavlensky, Ann, et al., *The Great Learning Book.* Reading, Mass.: Addison-Wesley, 1977.

A resource and idea book that suggests ways of bringing the world into the classroom. It provides a fund of possible writing experiences.

Bradley, Buff, with the editors of *Learning Magazine, Growing From Word Play Into POETRY.* Palo Alto, Calif.: Education Today Company, Inc., 1976.

Classroom activities to motivate and develop creative-writing skills, insights, projects, and ideas.

Brown, Rosellen, et al., *The Whole World Catalogue I.* New York: Teachers & Writers Collaborative, 1972.

A collection of writing ideas and directions for elementary and secondary students; with an annotated bibliography.

Cheyney, Arnold B., *The Writing Corner.* Santa Monica, Calif.: Goodyear, 1979.

A practical book that includes ideas on writing letters and reports and stimulating creative efforts. It includes fifty-three reproducible worksheets and activities.

Christensen, Fred, *Springboards To Creative Writing.* Monterey Park, Calif.: Creative Teaching Press, Inc., 1971.

This book is filled with story starters and ideas to motivate all types of creative writing.

Connolly, Francis, *The Types of Literature.* Harcourt, Brace and Company, 1955.

A text that covers the short story, novel, poetry, drama, essay, and criticism; gives an excellent theoretical analysis of each, with many selected works by established writers.

Cramer, Ronald, L., *Children's Writing and Language Growth.* Bell & Howell Company, 1978.

A "how-to" teacher's book of ideas, methods, and examples for teaching and involving children in writing.

Frank, Marjorie, *If You're Trying To Teach Kids To Write, You've Gotta Have This Book!* Nashville: Incentive Publications, Inc., 1979.

This book is filled with advice and information for teaching and involving students in creative writing. Numerous ideas for all kinds of writing activities and experiences; there is an annotated bibliography.

Hennings, Dorothy Grant, *Communication in Action: Dynamic Teaching of the Language Arts.* Chicago: Rand McNally, 1978.

A very comprehensive, practical, and idea-filled book on teaching the language arts; with sections on developing writing skills and creative writing.

Hook, J.N., *Writing Creatively.* Lexington, Mass.: Heath, 1967.

One of the best advice and information books I've come across. It goes into detail helping the reader understand each form of creative writing, including poetry, essay, and fiction. It gives activities for students to do.

Lewis, Claudia, *A Big Bite of the World: Children's Creative Writing.* Englewood Cliffs, N.J.: Prentice-Hall, 1979.

An idea-filled book to help motivate students to write. It includes ways to get quiet children to express themselves.

Lopate, Phil, *Being With Children.* New York: Doubleday, 1975.

The book has practical suggestions for teaching writing, theater, and video production and describes a "team" approach to teaching the arts.

Sealey, Leonard, et al., *Children's Writing: An Approach for the Primary Grades.* Newark, Delaware: International Reading Association, Inc., 1979.

Ideas and activities on how to get children to write.

Wermuth, Linda, *Imagination and Language.* Englewood Cliffs, N.J.: Prentice-Hall, 1976.

Writing-skill activities and use of imagination for upper elementary- and junior-high-school students are found in this book; pages can be duplicated.

Zavatsky, Bill, and Padgett, Ron, editors. *The Whole World Catalogue 2.* New York: McGraw-Hill Paperbacks, published in association with Teachers & Writers Collaborative, 1977.

A collection of ideas and materials to stimulate creativity in the classroom; it includes an annotated bibliography.

selected bibliography

ANDERSON, PAUL S. *Language Skills in Elementary Education,* 2nd edition. New York: The Macmillan Company, 1972.

APPLEGATE, MAUREE. *Helping Children Write.* Evanston, Illinois: Row, Peterson and Company, 1961.

BATES, JEFFERSON D. *Writing With Precision,* 2nd edition. Washington, D.C.: Acropolis Books Ltd., 1978.

BLAKE, JIM and BARBARA ERNST. *The Great Perpetual Learning Machine.* Boston-Toronto: Little, Brown and Company, 1976.

BOYD, GERTRUDE A. *Teaching Communication Skills In The Elementary Schools.* New York: D. Van Nostrand Company, 1970.

BURNS, PAUL C., J. ESTILL ALEXANDER and ARNOLD R. DAVIS. *Language Arts Concepts For Elementary School Teachers.* Itasca, Illinois: F.E. Peacock Publishers, Inc., 1972.

CHRISTENSEN, FRED. *Springboards to Creative Writing.* Monterey Park, California: Creative Teaching Press, Inc., 1971.

CLEGG, A.B. *The Excitement of Writing.* New York: Schocken Books, 1972.

CONNOLLY, FRANCIS. *The Types of Literature.* New York: Harcourt, Brace and Company, 1955.

DAY, ROBERT ed. *Creative Writing in the Classroom: An Annotated Bibliography of Selected Resources.* Urbana, Illinois: National Council of Teachers of English, 1978.

FOX, ROBERT ed. *Good Old Poems/I Love Them—An Anthology.* Columbus, Ohio: Ohio Foundation on the Arts for the Ohio Arts Council, 1979.

FRANK, MAJORIE. *If You're Trying To Teach Kids To Write You've Gotta Have This Book.* Nashville: Incentive Publications, 1979.

HENNINGS, DOROTHY GRANT. *Communication in Action—Dynamic Teaching of the Language Arts.* Chicago: Rand McNally College Publishing Company, 1978.

HENNINGS, DOROTHY and BARBARA ERNST. *Content and Craft—Written Expression in the Elementary School.* Englewood Cliffs, New Jersey: Prentice-Hall, Inc., 1973.

HOOK, J.N. *Writing Creatively,* 2nd edition. Boston: D.C. Heath and Company, 1967.

LEWIS, CLAUDIA. *A Big Bite of the World.* Englewood Cliffs, New Jersey: Prentice-Hall, Inc., 1979.

LOPATE, PHILLIP. *Being With Children.* Garden City, New York: Doubleday & Company, Inc., 1975.

LOS ANGELES UNIFIED SCHOOL DISTRICT. *Life is a Wonder.* Los Angeles: An area 9 publication by Elementary Students, 1979.

LUNDSTEEN, SARA W. ed. *Help for the Teacher of Written Composition.* Urbana, Illinois: ERIC—Clearinghouse on Reading and Communication Skills, 1976.

MORGAN, THOMAS. *The Basics of Creativity and the Arts.* Southern California Institute Press, 1974.

MURPHY, RICHARD. *Imaginary Worlds—Notes on a New Curriculum.* New York: A Virgil Book published by Teachers and Writers Collaborative, 1974.

PERCY, BERNARD. *How To Grow A Child . . . A Child's Advice to Parents.* Los Angeles: Price, Stern and Sloan, Inc., 1978.

PETTY, WALTER T., DOROTHY C. PETTY and MARJORIE F. BECKING. *Experiences in Language—Tools and Techniques for Language Arts Methods.* Boston: Allyn and Bacon, Inc., 1973.

PRATT-BUTLER, GRACE K. *Let Them Write Creatively.* Columbus, Ohio: Charles E. Merrill Publishing Company, 1973.

SOLARI, CAM SMITH ed. *Our Class Book—The Greatest Stories in the World.* Los Angeles: Cam Smith Solari Publisher, 1975.

STAUDACHER, CAROL. *Creative Writing in the Classroom.* Belmont, California: Fearon Publishers, 1968.

WEINER, HARVEY S. *Any Child Can Write—How to Improve Your Child's Writing Skills from Preschool through High School.* New York: McGraw-Hill Book Company, 1978.

ZAVATSKY, BILL and RON PADGETT eds. *The Whole Word Catalogue 2.* New York: McGraw-Hill Paperbacks (published in association with Teachers & Writers Collaborative), 1977.

index